PRAISE FOR ESPIRITISMO

"Hector Salva brings the luz (light) to a proud and beautiful tradition in his newest book, *Espiritismo: Puerto Rican Mediumship and Magic*. He intertwines his personal experiences as an *espiritisto* with a compelling narrative of the history and practices of this longstanding, yet often misunderstood, practice. Techniques, traditions, and praise for the blessings one can achieve through spiritual evolution can be found in this book, alongside blunt warnings about the dangers one may find in the spirit world via direct examples illustrating the power and tremendous responsibility that a medium bears. Just as the *espiritisto* elevates their ancestors and spirits in search of Universal Light, so Hector elevates readers through this book which honors his Boriquen ancestors and their evolving Espiritismo traditions."

—Mambo Chita Tann, author of *Haitian Vodou*

"Papa Hector Salva has outdone himself with *Espiritismo*. This is a one-of-a-kind book and a must-read. So much knowledge and information are shared within these pages. I love the stories of his youth. Papa Hector explains things in a way that even a novice can understand."

—Starr Casas, author of *Old Time Conjure and Hoodoo Your Love*

"Hector Salva's *Espiritismo* combines cultural, historical, and personal experiences to bring readers into the world of Puerto Rican Espiritismo. Salva's narratives take you into the reading rooms of mediums where you swear you can smell the incense and feel the presence of the sacred. *Espiritismo* introduces readers to the spirits of the *Gitanas, Santos,* and *Indios,* as it demonstrates the fascinating diversity of the tradition. An insightful contribution to the field of cultural understanding."

—Tony Kail, cultural anthropologist and author
of *A Secret History of Memphis Hoodoo*

T0046344

"In *Espiritismo*, Hector Salva recounts with sentiment and love the spiritualism he grew up with in Puerto Rico. I certainly can relate to a lot of similarities with the spiritual praxis of my own roots from my native Cuba. As Salva speaks of working with the ALL and the spirits, I am reminded of the primordial force that binds us all. I admire Salva's writings about the "Science of the Spirit"—knowledge being a key component of consciousness, which is spirit and soul. An exceptional read filled with informative material and wisdom, *Espiritismo* is truly a worthy addition to anyone's spiritual library.

—Reverend Alexander Cabot, author of *Touched by the Goddess*

"*Espiritismo* compiles folk history and the author's stories of his personal experiences with the magic and folklore of Puerto Rico. *Espiritismo* is another magnificent work of traditional spiritism from Papa Hector, written from the point of view of a true expert with the heart of a warrior who is here to teach you and guide you to work your own powerful sorcery in a new and different direction"

—Elhoim Leafar, author of *The Magical Art of Crafting Charm Bags* and *Manifestation Magic*

ESPIRITISMO

ESPIRITISMO

Puerto Rican Mediumship and Magic

HECTOR SALVA

WEISER BOOKS

This edition first published in 2022 by Weiser Books, an imprint of

Red Wheel/Weiser, LLC
With offices at:
65 Parker Street, Suite 7
Newburyport, MA 01950
www.redwheelweiser.com

ISBN: 978-1-57863-757-7

Library of Congress Cataloging-in-Publication Data available upon request.

Cover design by Kathryn Sky-Peck
Cover photograph © iStock
Interior by Debby Dutton
Typeset in Adobe Garamond and Frutiger LT,
Printed in the United States of America
IBI

10 9 8 7 6 5 4 3 2 1

Dedicated to God, the good spirits, Puerto Rico, and the Puerto Rican people. May God and the good spirits bring you life everlasting.

CONTENTS

ACKNOWLEDGMENTS

Thank you to Mama Juana and everyone and everything that has healed, guided, and assisted me throughout this beautiful journey called Life. I also want to thank everyone who has supported me and the Great Work. Without you, there would be no me.

PREFACE

The principles of faith, hope, and charity form the foundation of the guiding values that Espiritistas strive to channel. Their purpose is to live in faith of the Divine, to act as a fountain of hope for others and for themselves, and to be generous, kind, and compassionate toward all.

Faith in what we know to be true confers strength and, where strength exists, weakness cannot. True faith burns like a fire in the heart of those who know what they know and move forward in strength on that knowledge. Where faith exists, fear cannot enter.

Hope is the driving force of life. It is what keeps us pushing, alive, growing, and wanting more. Without hope, humanity would have become extinct long ago. Many have been saved by the power of hope alone. Many have been lifted by her gentle hand from the deepest of ditches. Many have found their way out of the depths illuminated by just a glimpse of her strength-giving light.

Through charity, we help others progress on their spiritual paths and develop their connection to the Divine. Through charity, we encourage both faith and hope. Through charity, we manifest love.

—Message from the enlightened spirits via Papa Hector

INTRODUCTION

Everywhere truth, you just have to find it.
—*Doña Juana, Espiritista*

You are about to start an incredible journey into the spiritual world—a journey of wisdom and empowerment, a journey into a deep part of yourself, a journey that will unlock and open doors into a world of beauty and mystery that consists of much more than just what the eye can see. In fact, Puerto Rican Espiritismo is a spiritual practice that is designed to open the many realms of existence to you. Its practices can help you grow on all levels and encourage you to experience life in ways that will strengthen and clarify your connection to the Divine. Its wisdom nurtures you and gives you understanding of life and beyond that can help you find wholeness. Its principles form a complete philosophy of balance, wellness, and health.

The teachings of Espiritismo are the same as those found in all teachings of Truth. This same wisdom can be found in all traditions, religions, and sects. Espiritismo merely distills this wisdom into its purest form. That is why I often refer to it as the "Science of the Spirit."

My own spiritual journey down this path began at birth. I was born and raised in a family of *espiritistas*. At one time, almost every member of my family was a practitioner of Espiritismo or some related form of spirituality. In fact, my entire family history weaves together a story of struggle, beauty, life, and magic.

Espiritismo has always been and still is part of my daily life. Its truths have guided me spiritually from the very beginning and continue to do so now. The wisdom that I gained from growing up in Espiritismo has helped me throughout my entire life journey and granted me understanding where others found only confusion. It has been the foundational vehicle through which I was able to reach total awakening and enlightenment.

I grew up with my maternal grandmother, who was a well-known *espiritista* and healer. She ran a full-time healing practice while raising a bunch of grandkids and adopted children and pursuing her own divine mission of "feeding the people." A normal day in our home consisted of her cooking more than ten pounds of food as she consulted with and healed people at our dining room table.

As well as being practitioners of Espiritismo, we were also members of a Pentecostal church. If you know anything about Pentecostalism, then you know that this appears to be a huge contradiction. But there were reasons for this odd mix of faiths. In fact, this spiritual mix is not uncommon in Puerto Rican families, as you will discover.

My grandfather had become a Pentecostal Christian quite some time before I was born, and this conversion totally changed his life. My grandmother supported him wholeheartedly in this, often saying: "It was the best thing that happened to him, when he accepted Christ." His new faith changed my grandfather from an alcoholic womanizer—albeit a hard-working man—to a loyal, faithful, and sober person. It gave him a sense of stability and a moral compass. Amazingly, he never tried to push his newfound connection with the Divine on my grandmother. As he put it: "When I met her, she was already more of a saint than a human being, more of a nun than the nuns."

My grandfather feared but respected the spirits and my grandmother's traditional practices. His own mother was an *espiritista* and healer, and he had grown up around the work, so he fully supported all my grandmother's desires and contributed to her mission of feeding people. He even bought healing items for people when they couldn't afford them and helped my grandmother maintain her healing garden and all the plants and herbs she used in her practices.

Surprisingly, my grandmother was a highly active and well-respected member of my father's church as well. She became an elder and her counsel was regularly sought in all important matters. In fact, no big decisions were ever taken without her input, even though it was well known by all that she was an *espiritista*. This church, she said, was "better than the Catholics because you get to have the Holy Spirit." Pentecostals believe in possession and messages delivered via the Holy Spirit, and highly value the gift of "speaking in tongues."

As my grandmother often said: "God is everywhere—at home and at the church." So it was common for us to attend *reuniones espirituales* (*espiritista* rituals) on Friday or Saturday night and attend church on Sunday, Tuesday, and Thursday. Yes, God and Spirit were #1 in my household growing up. When speaking about it, I often joke that it was a full-time job!

This intense spirituality, however, instilled in me the capacity to see how important the Divine really is in life. In fact, some people endure incredible amounts of suffering daily simply because they lack this personal connection to the Divine. Illnesses, emotional and mental problems, and issues in relationships all have a spiritual component and reflect an imbalance that could so easily be corrected if the Divine were present.

In my grandmother's home, it was normal for people to start showing up for spiritual help any time after 8:00 in the morning. In fact, they showed up at all hours of the day or night, especially in emergencies. Once there, they were usually invited to have some coffee or juice as they waited until my grandmother was ready to attend to them. Our dining room table was not just for eating; it was a center for healing, love, connection, and much more. She sat people down there and consulted with them. Sometimes she asked them to bring something back so she could help them. Sometimes she referred them to other spiritual workers who were specialists in the issues they needed to resolve. And sometimes, she simply told them what they needed the moment she saw them.

As all of this was going on, this remarkable lady had huge pots of rice and meats cooking. The smells of the delicious food permeated the whole house. If the food was done, people were invited to share it. My grandmother's mission was not just to nourish the spirit, but to feed the body as well. And we also regularly had people who needed help staying with us. Every evening, mats, quilts, and blankets were brought out to make up pallets for those in need. In our house, you frequently had to jump over people to get from one place to another at night. It was not uncommon for us to have more than a dozen people staying with us at any given point.

In addition to my grandmother, several of my paternal great-aunts, uncles, and cousins were practicing *espiritistas* as well. Many of them practiced Sanse Espiritismo, a related type of spirituality. Two of them led *centros* or spiritual centers, where they regularly held spiritual rituals. Some were involved in the 21 Divisions, a Dominican spiritual tradition. Others were involved in Santeria, a

Cuban spiritual path. As I said, spirituality and religiosity were a basic component of my family life.

PUERTO RICAN *ESPIRITISMO*

The history of Puerto Rico and its many people is like a quilt, with many different types of fabric that have been sewn together. Over time, many cultures left their imprint on Puerto Rico, including their spiritual imprint. The island became home to many refugees, as well as a place to which many came for commerce and for a chance to better their lives. One result of this cultural merging is Espiritismo, a Spanish word that means Spiritism. Espiritismo is a spiritual path of development and mediumship that incorporates a belief in one God and in a spiritual world that contains many spirits, both incarnate and disincarnate, who affect each other and us.

Espiritismo is often referred to as *la Obra*, or the Work—not just any work, but the sacred work of God. *Espiritistas* function as a channel for God, for *la luz* (the light), and for the spirits of healing and good. The focus of this sacred work is the path of development.

Most Puerto Rican *espiritistas* are Catholic in background, although this is not a requirement and there are *espiritistas* from various other religious backgrounds as well. Some are Protestant, some are Muslim, and some are even scientists. In fact, during its period of growth, many different types of Espiritismo were formed. Most practitioners do not even consider Espiritismo to be a religion. They see it rather as a spiritual practice of development that can complement any religion. In fact, the truths of Espiritismo, properly understood, are the underlying truths of all religions. Its teachings are universal.

Puerto Rican Espiritismo combines elements of Catholicism, Protestantism, various indigenous native spiritualities, shamanism,

European Spiritism and Spiritualism, New Age spirituality, and more. It was birthed on the island of Puerto Rico where, as you'll see, many diverse influences came together to form the culture, the traditions, and the people. All these influences are reflected within Espiritismo.

Puerto Rican Espiritismo teaches that the goal of life is to come closer to God by undergoing the process of *desarrollo*, or unravelment. It is grounded in the belief that the spiritual world and the physical world are interdependent and interactive. Thus, by practicing and participating in an active spiritual life, we can affect and improve our physical existence. Since many of our problems are caused by being apart from the Divine, we can improve our lives by drawing closer to the Divine.

Espiritismo also teaches that faith, hope, charity, forgiveness, love, empathy, and gratitude are the ways to live a healthy life. It encourages the development of high ethical and moral values that act as a guide to its practitioners. Through its practices, we can enrich our lives and our souls. Espiritismo is grounded in beliefs and practices that are needed to live a successful life. As a healing tradition, it works in a holistic way to heal people on all levels. In fact, all levels of the human experience are addressed by Espiritismo.

Puerto Rican Espiritismo is also known as Mesa Blanca, meaning "white table," because its foundational ritual, known as a *reunion espiritual*, or spiritual reunion, is conducted on a table covered by a white cloth. During this ritual, practitioners known as *espiritistas* communicate and interact with the spiritual world and with spirits to convey their messages to the living who are present. In this process, healing can occur, wisdom can be dispensed, and lessons can be learned.

There is a wide range of skill among *espiritistas*, as well as a wide range of depth to their practices. Some are more casually involved;

others are very deeply committed. Some are mediums who can communicate and interact with the spirit world and thus act as vehicles for healing. Some mediums known as *brujos* can work with the spiritual world to create miracles and change for others.

In Espiritismo, there is no grand hierarchal structure. Instead, its practitioners are recognized for the level of development of their spiritual abilities. The more developed an *espiritista*, the more "elder" he or she is in relation to others. These elders are often called *mayores* or *viejos*—the old ones.

The tradition of Espiritismo is transmitted via apprenticeship that includes study and training, as well as personal and group rituals. Apprentices undergo healings, spiritual development, and other personal practices. Master teachers are known as *padrinos* (male) and *madrinas* (female), while students are called *ahijados,* or godchildren.

WHY I WROTE THIS BOOK

Right now, a powerful awakening is underway. People are becoming more and more conscious. Many old restrictions or ways of being that prevented people from opening up are falling away. Right now, the wisdom of Espiritismo is needed by people more than ever before. In our fast-moving and disconnected society, we need to maintain our connection to the Divine more than ever to make our lives joyous.

Espiritismo provides the foundational and universal wisdom that can give us that connection. Its truths are applicable to all. It doesn't require that anyone change their religion or their beliefs. Rather, it gives a clarifying, penetrating knowledge of what Truth *is*. It can be practiced in harmony with any religion, or with no religion at all.

Espiritismo holds the Hermetic truth that what you seek is within you. You are divine and connected to the Divine in many ways. Its practices, teachings, and rituals can lead you to that truth.

Its wisdom and insights can lead you to enlightenment. In fact, it is one of the few paths outside of Eastern spiritualities and religions devoted to that goal.

Espiritismo holds fundamental spiritual truths and essential wisdom teachings that are slowly being lost. As people and cultures shift, morph, and change, they tend to lose sight of what is important and this causes unnecessary suffering. By recognizing the Truth and Spirit in all paths, Espiritismo offers a way out of this dilemma.

FROM DARKNESS INTO LIGHT

Tia Nereida always awoke bright and early, taking her time for a morning ritual that consisted of eating breakfast slowly, and methodically making herself up for the day while music played softly in the background.

"*Nene*, don't rush," she would say. "*En la vida*, there is time for everything. Time is my best friend; he waits upon me. We miss so much when we constantly obsess over getting things done."

"Tia, how did you become a *bruja*?" I asked.

"I was born one of course, just like you," she replied smiling.

"I mean, how did you know?" I countered.

"Ever since I can remember, I could see things," she began. "But I never told anyone, because my mother is a *bruja* and I didn't want to be one. I thought if I didn't talk about the visions, they would just stop. Then, when I was a teenager, I fell deeply in love with a gorgeous young man named Tomas and he fell in love with me. But my mother and father didn't approve of him. They said he was trouble. But I was always the hardheaded one, so we kept seeing one another and, eventually, I became pregnant with his child. My father was enraged, and my brothers wanted to fight him. My mother said nothing. My sisters were the only ones who were happy for me.

"Then one day, a friend of Tomas invited us over for a party. We went to his house and we had a great time. I remember it was a beautiful night; the moon was almost full and the sky was bright with stars. As Tomas and I got ready to leave, however, another man came up to us and accused Tomas of owing him some money. The argument slowly grew out of control and, in the end, Tomas was stabbed and killed. During the struggle, I was knocked to the ground on my belly. That night, I lost both Tomas and my baby. It was too much. I went into shock and, for the next week, descended into darkness—a darkness that was real and threatened to consume me."

Tia Nereida's face became profoundly serious. "It was very sad," she said. "But it is past. What matters is that that terrible night led me into darkness so that I could see the light—*la luz*. With the help of the spirits, I emerged from the darkness and began to see my power of sight as a blessing, not a curse. Now I use that power to help others."

Chapter 1

THE ROOTS OF PUERTO RICAN SPIRITUALITY

Puerto Rico is a small island in the Caribbean that measures only 110 miles long and thirty-five miles wide, making it roughly the size of the state of Connecticut. Made known to Europeans by Christopher Columbus during his voyages to the Western Hemisphere, the island was originally inhabited by the Taino Indians.

Tainos were a peace-loving people. In fact, the word *taino* means "friend" or "relative." Their culture was shamanic, grounded in a belief in the gods of nature, and their traditions were nature-based. In addition, they believed that everyone had a personal spirit guide who served and protected them.

The Taino gladly accepted the Spanish when they came to the island. But this ultimately led to their downfall. Many died of illnesses brought by the Spanish. Others were worked to death as slaves. Although the Taino were almost eradicated in other parts of the Caribbean, however, in Puerto Rico, many Taino women were taken as wives by the Spanish. Thus many of their native healing practices survived with them and were passed down to later generations. These practices later became a major influence in Puerto Rican Espiritismo.

Many Spanish who came to the island came to find a better life. They were ambitious and wanted to improve their lot. In Spain, they were hampered by a class system dominated by the elite. For them, Puerto Rico was a land of opportunity, and the Tainos welcomed them with open arms into a society that was communal. No one owned anything; everything belonged to the whole group. Only two members of each village had their own belongings—the *cacique,* or chief, and the shaman.

The Spanish quickly began to enslave the naive and friendly Tainos. Many of them died. When they finally recognized the danger that the Spanish represented and tried to resist, it was too late and they were cruelly oppressed. The Spanish had guns and many other weapons that the Taino didn't have, so they were ultimately successful in their conquest of the island and its people.

The Spanish killed off many of the Taino men. But they hadn't brought their wives and children with them from Spain, so they took the Taino women, who were reputed to be incredibly beautiful, for their own. After they had been on the island for some time, they began having children with these women and started to establish families there. The children of these families came to be known as *Criollos* or Creoles. Although by virture of their Spanish parentage these children generally belonged to the middle and upper classes, they were not afforded the same rights as those who were of pure European blood.

The Taino mothers made sure to teach their children the old ways. They continued to use plants to heal and taught their children how to find their "stone of power" and how to live and work in the mountains. They passed the traditional songs and stories along to them. But they also adopted the Catholic saints that the Spanish had brought with them, fashioning statues of them made of wood just as they did for their own nature gods. In time, the Spanish ways and the old Taino ways mingled, and the songs and stories came to represent a bit of both cultures.

Over time, the Taino people became less and less sure of who they were. The old ways faded and were in danger of being lost. The gods of nature disappeared behind the Catholic saints. Their language slowly began to disappear. Although some vestiges remained, the friendly communal society of the Taino foundered. Taino turned on Taino and the greed of the invaders took hold.

According to the history books, the Taino were completely wiped out, eradicated by the Europeans. Yet members of my family claim this is untrue. And indeed, recent studies have shown that Puerto Ricans have more than 60 percent Taino DNA, with the rest made up of varying amounts of Spanish and West African heritage—more than any other part of the Caribbean (see *wearemitu.com*). The Taino DNA that is carried by Puerto Ricans today comes from the maternal line, indicating that we received it from the Taino women taken as wives by the Spanish. It has also recently been discovered that the reason the Tainos were thought to have "disappeared" was that the Spanish dropped the classification on the census in 1800. In 1899, however, when the United States acquired the island, they did a new census that showed that more than 80 percent of the people in the interior of the island appeared to be of native blood or native blood mixed with either European or African blood. So the Taino did not really disappear; they were assimilated.

Because of this, many survived who treasured the ways of old and they kept their traditions alive as much as they could. It wasn't easy, and much was lost as each new generation moved farther and farther from their roots. But as my *bisabuela,* my great-grandmother, used to say: "Memories are weak, my son, and they don't get better with time. And yet here we are, the *Indios de Borinquen* (Puerto Rico)."

THE AFRICAN INFLUENCE

Starting in the early 1500s, the Spanish began using Puerto Rico as a port for the trafficking of slaves throughout the Western Hemisphere, it being a mid-point in their journey west. Yet, although many slaves were trafficked through Puerto Rico, only a small number of them stayed there at this time. Unlike many of the other islands in the Caribbean, Puerto Rico didn't really acquire a large African population until the early to mid-1800s, and, even then, the African population there remained quite small in comparison to most of the other islands. In fact, it never exceeded 10 percent. This is vastly different from other Caribbean islands, many of whose populations were more than 40 percent African.

Like the Taino, the various African tribes brought to Puerto Rico each had their own religious and spiritual traditions. Of all the slaves brought to the island, it's estimated that the majority, more than 80 percent, were of Congo-Bantu origin. And the Kongo, as they were called, believed in a cosmology much like that of the Taino. They believed in a creator deity and in divinities grounded in nature, as well as in personal guides who assisted individuals throughout life. But by the time a significant number of these slaves began to stay in Puerto Rico, the Spanish had already settled in and brought their culture and beliefs to bear on the older Taino ways. The Catholic Church and its program of conversion were well established. As a result, Puerto Rico retained less of the African religions than many of the other Caribbean islands.

SPANISH CATHOLICS

The Spanish were strongly Catholic and very connected to the Catholic Church at the time of the conquest of Puerto Rico. In fact, from the beginning of their settling there, the Catholic Church ruled the island. Unfortunately, they made it their mission to eradicate the beliefs of the Taino, and eventually of the slaves. The control and influence of the Church was particularly strong in Puerto Rico. At one time, the island had 365 Catholic churches—one for every day of the year. Thus the process of converting the natives, and later the slaves, to Catholicism was a matter of policy and was closely monitored. Unlike on other islands of the Caribbean, the Church kept a watchful eye on the conversion of both the Taino and the Africans.

They were relatively successful in these conversion efforts and managed to eradicate many of the old beliefs. But the mountainous and rural nature of the island allowed many of the new Creole and old Taino people to keep personal shrines with carved statues of wooden saints known as *santos de bulto*. In many cases, these saints replaced the faces and names of the old gods, but they continued to work in just the same way that the Taino gods had. The ancient Taino healing practices, medicines, and techniques continued to be used and, with the help of these hybrid saints, the old magic remained powerful in their hands.

In Puerto Rico, as in the rest of the Caribbean, these three cultures—the Spanish, the Taino, and the African—came together and blended. In time, since the island was a common destination for refugees, other cultures also became mingled in. And this is the spiritual stew in which Puerto Rican Espiritismo born.

A TAINA WHO NEVER FORGOT

Whenever she visited, *mi bisabuela*, my great-grandmother, received many visitors. Each day was filled with familiar friends and family members, as well as others who were totally unknown to me. They came simply to pay their respects or to show her their children or grandchildren. Doña Juana was a retired spiritual healer, and many of those who came to see her had been helped by her in some way or another throughout her long career. During her visits to our house, we also often made rounds visiting various people she had known.

She spoke the old tongue, the Taino words, just like the native inhabitants of the island. Every morning, she sat in a rocking chair on the front porch, a chair that had been bought just for her visits some years back. When she left, it was kept in the basement, where no one could touch it, much less sit in it.

As she rocked in her chair, with the sun pouring onto the side of her face, she sipped coffee and hummed a tune—a tune that was sweet and sad at the same time, with a hypnotizing rhythm. Over and over she hummed it, while staring into the street before her.

Noticing that I was watching her from the window as I ate my hot *surullos* (cornbread sticks with cheese), my grandfather said: "*Sabes quien es?* Do you know who she is?"

I nodded my head yes.

"Go speak with her," he insisted, prodding me gently. "She's only here for a few months." So off I went to see what she would say. As I came out the door, she looked at me and a huge smile shone upon her face.

"*Igualito igualito a el,*" Doña Juana said. "Exactly, but so exactly like him," telling me that I looked exactly like her husband, now deceased, my great-grandfather. In fact, people had reminded me more than a dozen times of this in the last few days since my great-grandmother had arrived. He was the reason I have hazel eyes, or so they tell me.

"*Nene* (child), come here," she said, pressing me up against her, hugging me, and sitting me in her lap. I held up some of my own weight, afraid I might be too heavy for her to lift. "Relax," she said. And, facing a clear open sky and warmed by the sunshine, she began to speak.

"In Puerto Rico, when I awaken, I sit on the porch looking at *las montañas*, the mountains. There I sing to the birds, and they come down. I call them, and birds of every color come down the mountain. They surround my little house and make miracles."

"How do you call them?" I asked. "What colors are they?"

"They are beautiful, brilliant, bright colors," she replied. "You don't have them around here. Red, yellow, and green. There are birds of one color, two colors, and many colors. But they aren't from here. I called them for you before when you were younger and at my house. Do you remember?"

Vaguely at first, and then more and more clearly, I remembered being at her house in Puerto Rico and seeing it surrounded by many birds. I remembered how colorful and vibrant they were. I just had never known how or why they were there. Confirming my memory, I nodded vigorously and said: "But how do you call them?"

"With a song of course."

"Just like that?" I asked, attempting to snap my fingers and failing.

"No, it's not just any song. It is a special song that my mother taught me, a song of the Taino."

"So, your mom was a Taina," I asked, puzzled.

"Yes," she replied, looking deeply into the sky. "And I am too. We are *jibaros*, you know? We know the power of the Earth and its beauty."

Noticing a group of crows, I asked: "Can you call those birds here?"

"Sure, but they are not my birds. I would rather watch them and see what they do. Let's not disturb them."

"Will you teach me the song?" I asked.

"One day, but you're too young now, and it's not just a game. If you sing the song, you must know why you are doing it. Never do things just to do them. You have to have an incredibly good reason for it."

"Can you tell me about the Taino?" I asked, moving deeper into her warmth.

"Of course," she replied. "Long ago, our beautiful island was the home of the *Indios*, who were called Tainos. They were beautiful people, slender, with beautiful eyes and a warm spirit." She blinked her eyes widely.

"They were an innocent pure people. Simple and humble people. They had respect. All over the island they had their chiefs, called *caciques*. The chiefs made sure there was peace with the people, and that they had what they needed. They were healthy and strong. They were incredibly enchanting, which is why we are called the island of enchantment. They weren't rich in money, but in their souls they had a great abundance. They were good people. Clean people. But they were no match for the Spanish. The Spanish were not clean."

"They didn't bathe?" I wondered.

"No child; they bathed. But their hearts were dirty. Hearts don't wash with soap, my son. Ambition, greed, and jealousy are stains that don't come out just like that. That's what was wrong with the Spanish.

"When I was a girl," she continued, "whenever you could hear drums, no one could find me. They would look and look, but they would not be able to find me anywhere. Eventually, they learned that, if they could hear the drums, that's where they should look. And no matter how far away the drums were beating, I could hear them clearly. Many times, I was found miles away from my house.

"When I got to where the drums were, I hid in the trees watching. Often, someone saw me and invited me over. Standing at the edge of a circle, I could see people around a big bonfire. Some were dancing around it, and some were eventually possessed. The spirit Chango took them over and they started flailing their limbs. Yelling and jumping, sometimes.

"But I was never afraid. In fact, I loved it. When the spirit overtook them, their eyes burned with fire. I loved it when Chango came on the people. He often rubbed them down and talked with them, and sometimes he danced. Then he sat near the fire and people brought him food. Many times, he poured the food on the ground, then mixed it with dirt and ate it. Sometimes he threw some of it in the fire.

"Everyone there was nice and generous with each other. I was always offered food. People were usually talking and laughing around the edges of the circle and children were playing. It was always nice, but what I was always most drawn to was Chango and the dancing and the drums.

"The drums—the drums. They just called to me, my son. This was probably my first real step into the spiritual world. But I did not know at the time that one day I would also serve the spirits. It wasn't till later that I became sick and was healed by an *espiritista*. And that was how my own journey into the spirit world began."

Chapter 2

THE BIRTH OF ESPIRITISMO

In the mid-1800s, Spain issued a law that gave people a greater degree of personal religious freedom than ever before. Across Europe, the Catholic Church was losing some of its hold over people as well. As a result, freemasonry societies, esoteric schools, and Spiritualism gained popularity all over the continent. It was at this time that a new philosophy and esoteric spiritualistic practice known as Spiritism (Espiritismo in Spanish) emerged.

Spiritism shared many of the aspects of Spiritualism. It provided a method of communicating with the spirit world. Both practices used séances to communicate with spirits from the "other side." The difference between them was the purpose of those communications. Spiritists also believed in one God, the reincarnation of spirits, various planes of existence, and the ability of spirits to interact with people. They focused on the power of this communication and interaction to help humanity develop consciously and socially.

Spiritism teaches that certain individuals have or can develop the powers to communicate with the spirit world. These individuals are known as mediums, or *espiritistas*, and they communicate with the spirits through séances—meetings at which people attempt to contact the dead or the spirits in order to get answers from the "other side." These séances came to be known as *sessiones* in Spanish.

Among its practitioners, Spiritism was considered the "scientific" method of spirit communication. Thus, it was not regarded as a religion at all, but rather as a new wave of science. In fact, in the early years of Espiritismo, many Spiritist sessions were led by medical doctors, lawyers, journalists, and other intellectuals. It was, in effect, the forerunner of what is now called parapsychology—the study of mental phenomena that are inexplicable by orthodox scientific means. This includes hypnosis, telepathy, psychic gifts, and other methods.

Professor and researcher Allen Kardec is generally recognized as the founder of Spiritism. Although not a medium himself, Kardec compiled the findings of many other mediums. He taught that Spiritism was a philosophy that presented a new view of the world and codified it as a method of research into the evolution of man. Although Spiritism was not a religion, he claimed, it could give people a deeper understanding of spiritual things. Thus, at first it wasn't considered a major threat by the Catholic Church. Kardec's form of Spiritism was also known as Scientific Spiritism.

In the mid-1800s, many wealthy families in Puerto Rico started sending their children to universities back in Europe. The island simply couldn't provide access to the educational resources that were available there. In Europe, these children were exposed to the teachings of Kardec and brought them back to Puerto Rico.

Kardec's Spiritism proved to be a perfect fit for many of the upper- and middle-class Creole elites who had grown tired of the Catholic Church's political power. Although many were Catholic themselves, they sought freedom and socio-political progress that was not forthcoming from the Church. They wanted radical changes in the way society functioned and felt that Kardec's Scientific Spiritism could support that vision. The *espiritistas* who followed Kardec's teachings created many public hospitals, schools, community centers, and spiritual centers based on his principles. They introduced free or community-based centers for health and education. They also sought to bring social services to the public at large.

Kardec's Scientific Spiritism didn't reach only the island of Puerto Rico. In fact, it reached many of the other islands in the region and much of South America as well. Mexico, Brazil, Venezuela, Cuba, and many other countries have their own forms of Espiritismo that blended Kardec's philosophy with local influences. And many of these local variants have come to influence Puerto Rican Espiritismo as well.

In the mid-1870s, however, the freedom granted earlier in the century was withdrawn by the Church and the law restored its political power. The Catholic and Apostolic Religions were declared the new state religions in Puerto Rico. A new law was issued stating that ceremonies or public manifestations other than those of the state religion would not be permitted. People still managed to practice their religious beliefs in private, but the Church worked hard at shutting down Espiritismo on the island.

In 1898, the Spanish lost a war with America and ceded ownership of Puerto Rico to the United States in the Treaty of Paris. This ushered in a new era on the island that nullified the Church's political power. Thanks to this, Puerto Rican Espiritismo experienced a major growth spurt. By the 1920s, Kardec's books on Scientific Spiritism had outsold the Bible on the island. It was estimated at that time that 90 percent of all Puerto Ricans practiced Spiritism.

ESPIRITISMO COMES TO AMERICA

The last time Puerto Rico was free was long before the island ever got its name. The last time Puerto Ricans owned and governed themselves was before Columbus arrived. In fact, the people of *Borinquen* (the Taino name for the island) have been owned by other nations ever since. Puerto Rico's freedom disappeared with the Taino.

The American victory in the Spanish-American War made Puerto Rico a territory of the United States. In 1917, Puerto Ricans officially became United States citizens. This allowed them to travel back and forth to the mainland, and many of them, in fact, moved there. In the 1950s, due to the economic instability of the island, huge waves of Puerto Ricans moved to America, encouraged by both the US and Puerto Rican governments, in hopes of improving their economic lives. And they brought Espiritismo with them.

Of course, America was vastly different from these refugees' island home. Many of the spiritual tools and goods that *espiritistas* had used on the island were unavailable in New York and other cities where they moved. As a result, some set up *botanicas*, spiritual supply stores. Many practiced in the back of convenience stores, in people's living rooms, and in the back of the *botanicas* that first appeared in Spanish Harlem in New York City in the late 1950s to fill the needs of *espiritistas* and other Afro-Caribbean spiritualists. These shops carried all sorts of religious and spiritual supplies that were used by *espiritistas*—images of saints, relics, herbs, oils, and spiritual statues among them.

From Harlem, *botanicas* spread out across America and eventually made their way back to the islands. Soon, Espiritismo began to influence magical practices all over. And Espiritismo, being as absorbent as a sponge, also adopted many of the influences it encountered in America, eventually bringing those influences back to Puerto Rico as well.

Many *botanica* owners were *espiritistas* who, in the back of their shops or in separate spaces, offered consultations and other spiritual services. These spaces were also used to hold *veladas*, or spiritual rituals. In fact, these shops were often the first place that many non-Puerto Rican spiritualists, mystics, and occultists crossed paths with Espiritismo. Eventually, the ceremonies and rituals that took place there came to influence many Latin American spiritual practices, as they made their way back to other countries. And although this made for beautiful growth for Espiritismo, this didn't come without a cost.

In the United States, even within the Puerto Rican community, being an *espiritista* carried a stigma. It could make you a target of negativity. In fact, some saw Spiritist practices as a barrier to assimilation that was holding back the community as a whole and they were determined to cleanse them from the culture. My grandmother, for instance, recalled various times when she was fired from jobs because she was discovered to be an *espiritista*. Nevertheless, Puerto Rican Espiritismo survived.

Because of Espiritismo's open and eclectic nature, however, its deep influence on other spiritual cultures isn't always evident. Likewise, because it embraces evolution and growth, it absorbs the influences of other spiritual cultures. This can make it exceedingly difficult to see where one set of beliefs ends and another begins.

In New York, with the rise of *botanicas*, *espiritistas* were exposed to a great number of other spiritualities, including Cuban Santeria, Palo Mayombe, Haitian Vodou, European witchcraft, and New Age philosophies. These were all brought back to Puerto Rico as well, incorporating a great number of new elements and deities into the practices of many native practitioners. And Espiritismo's beliefs and practices were likewise incorporated in varying degrees by those following these other spiritualities.

MESA BLANCA

To eradicate the traditions of both the Taino and the Africans, the Catholic Church demonized their gods and rituals. They outlawed their practices and declared them all to be satanic, black magic, and the "work of the devil." Catholics referred to all these practices as *brujeria*, or witchcraft, and called all those who pursued them *brujos*, or witches. Sometimes they were also known as *curanderos* (healers).

Because of the Church's political power, those practicing these arts could face dire consequences. Although many natives were not true converts to the new Catholic faith, they nonetheless knew that resistance to the Church's power would most often be futile. So they co-opted the service of the Catholic saints. At first, this made Church leadership happy by convincing them that they had successfully realized their mission of conversion. On closer inspection, however, they found things to be different than they appeared.

In fact, the service of the saints became a means for native islanders to preserve their own beliefs and practices. Rather than reject Catholicism, they simply blended it into their own traditions. For instance, the practice of *novenas*, or nine-day prayers, worked equally well to petition the dead, the spirits, or the saints. The herbal knowledge, healing, and magic that were all part of their original culture were simply added into their practice of Catholicism. Of course, the Church was not happy about this and merely ramped up its war against these "evil" practices. The slave owners, however, remained unconcerned and unbothered by it all, regarding it all as just superstition. Although not ideal for them, the situation would have to do.

These hybrid practices were then passed down and taught to the island children. At first, the Catholic saints served as veneers—masks—for the old gods. Over time, however, they totally absorbed the old gods. For children who had been born into Catholicism, these boundaries became blurred and it became unclear to them

ESPIRITISMO

where one tradition started and the other ended. Indeed, many of those deemed *brujos* or said to be practicing *brujeria* were often some of the most devout Catholics.

The establishment and acceptance of Kardec's Scientific Spiritism, however, gave a new home to native *brujos* and *curanderos*. Although still not accepted or sanctioned by the Church, Kardec's brand of Spiritism provided a perfect place for these practices to continue without constant persecution.

In fact, native beliefs and Kardec's teachings already shared many similarities—a belief in one Supreme Being, God; a belief in a spirit world with varying levels of development; a belief that the spiritual world and the physical world influence each other and interact. Yet there were many ways in which Kardec's teachings did not align with or were directly contradictory to native practices and beliefs.

For example, Kardecist practices didn't address the problems of the common people or the issues and concerns they faced in life. Kardecists, many of whom were members of the upper and middle classes, focused on political and social change. They were concerned primarily with mental practices, social activism, enlightenment, and politics. These were things with which most of the population could not afford to be concerned, however. For the majority, they didn't provide the day-to-day help they needed. On the other hand, the native healing practices had always worked. But, realizing that a certain level of protection and acceptance was afforded to Kardec's brand of Spiritism, native healers adopted the term *Espiritismo,* and even incorporated some of Kardec's practices and terms as well.

For instance, *espiritistas* adopted the term *medium* for those who had the capacity to communicate with the spirits and work with the spirit world to heal and create miracles, although in native traditions these individuals had always been known as *brujos* or *curanderos*. They also adapted their practice of *veladas* and *sessiones*, making the table or altar the central focus and tool of the rituals. This adaptation became known as Mesa Blanca (White Table) Espiritismo, which eventually became the predominant strain of Spiritism on the island. The ancestral healing methods that had been preserved and handed down were incorporated into Mesa Blanca, including magical practices, herbalism, the use of talismans, and more. What had been called *brujeria*, or witchcraft, and *curanderismo*, or folk healing, both became a major part of Mesa Blanca. But for Mesa Blanca *espiritistas*, the purpose of communication with the spirits was to heal people, to resolve life's problems, and to gain guidance. For them, illness and life's problems were caused by negative energies in the spiritual world.

Mesa Blanca has also been known under many other names, including Espiritismo *Criollo*, or Creole Spiritism, because it is a blend and mix of all the spiritual wisdom and influences of the people of Puerto Rico. It was also known as Espiritismo *del Jibaro* (country person) because it was most popular among the rural population. It was called Espiritismo *Folklorico*, or Folkloric Spiritism, by Kardecist practitioners, and eventually became known as Popular Espiritismo, since most practitioners on the island followed its precepts.

A HOME FOR EVERYONE

Throughout Puerto Rico's history, the island has been a home to refugees from various backgrounds, all of whom have brought with them their own native religions and spiritualities. Because of its own adaptive origins, Mesa Blanca Espiritismo has been able to accept and absorb these different traditions.

Haitians settlers were living in Puerto Rico as early as the mid-1890s, and there are even a few accounts of them moving to the island prior to that. In fact, several famous *espiritistas* are said to have been of Haitian origin and some elements of Haitian Vodou became incorporated into Puerto Rican Espiritismo. Likewise, records indicate that Dominicans were living in Puerto Rico as early as the late 1800s and early 1900s. They brought with them their own religious practices known as the 21 Divisions, a magical shamanic tradition with a strong Catholic influence that works with spirits known as *los misterios,* deities of various African tribes that were preserved and continued to be served. Certain aspects of the 21 Divisions were also incorporated by Mesa Blanca *espiritistas.*

Perhaps the largest group of immigrants to come to Puerto Rico came from Cuba. In the early 1950s, while many Puerto Ricans were moving to the United States, a huge number of Cuban refugees were moving to both the island of Puerto Rico and the US mainland, where they often lived and worked in the same communities. And, of course, they all brought their native spirituality with them.

Unlike in Puerto Rico, however, slavery in Cuba lasted longer and the percentage of the population with African ancestry was thus higher. As a result, the various religious traditions of the slaves were preserved to a greater degree. Two of the most important of these traditions were Santeria and Palo Mayombe. Santeria, also known as Lucumi, focuses on the deities, beliefs, and rituals of the Yoruba people of Africa, whose deities are known as *orishas*. Palo Mayombe, on the other hand, focuses on the religious practices of the Kongo who were enslaved in Cuba. Although Catholicism was incorporated to some degree in both of these traditions, in many ways it functioned only as a veneer for the old African faiths.

Both Santeria and Palo Mayombe retained many African religious elements, including their framework, their practices, and their worldview. Like the African traditions from which they sprang, they have their own ritual languages, their own practices, and their own initiation rituals. Both employ a priesthood and recognize a hierarchy and ranking among their practitioners. Another practice brought by the Cubans is Espiritismo Cruzado, which blended the native elements in Cuba with Santeria and Palo Mayombe. Most practitioners of Santeria and Palo Mayombe also practice some form of Espiritismo Cruzado. In fact, for many it is a prerequisite.

Both on the island and elsewhere, as Puerto Rican *espiritistas* started to cross paths with Cuban spiritualists, their traditions affected the development of Mesa Blanca. While there were also traditionalist *espiritistas* who flat out rejected all influences from Santeria, these were few in number. Early on, many Mesa Blanca practitioners incorporated many of the spirits of Santeria, as well as some of its healing practices. Since Puerto Rico hadn't retained as many African elements, many saw this as a way to develop their own connections with their African guides, roots, and heritage. Like their ancestors before them, they started incorporating these spirits, but they always approached them in ways that honored and preserved their own traditions, as opposed to how they were traditionally approached in Santeria.

Cuban Espiritismo incorporated some beliefs and practices that were at odds with those of Puerto Rican Espiritismo, however. For instance, *santeros* (priests of Santeria) saw their development as *espiritistas* as only a step toward being initiated as priests. This created a hierarchy in which they saw themselves as being "above" *espiritistas*. In turn, this changed how they approached their spirituality, which became a race to reach certain initiations, titles, and positions rather than a process of unending development. Rather than acting as starting points, these initiations became the final goal, Rather than working to develop their faculties through proper training, aspirants were tempted to buy them by purchasing ceremonies. By contrast, in Puerto Rican Espiritismo, no such hierarchy exists. Eldership is achieved through development, not initiation, and the only hierarchical relationship that exists is that between godparent (teacher) and godchild (student).

Many Mesa Blanca *espiritistas* still considered themselves religiously Catholic and foundationally *espiritistas*. They continued to hold a Catholic worldview, but most saw themselves as using it to enhance their traditional *protecciones,* or protections (see chapter 9), and *cuadros,* or spiritual frames (see chapter 5). They had no intention or desire to convert to a new religion. For them, their acceptance of Catholicism was an amplification of their old faith rather than a conversion to a new one.

Likewise, many aspects of Santeria didn't align with the tenets of Puerto Rican Espiritismo. For example, many traditional *espiritistas* saw no need to adopt foreign rituals, ceremonies, and initiations to work with the spirits. You either had the ability to work with the spirit world or you didn't. If you did, the spirits would respond to you. If not, they would simply ignore you. Mediumship was a gift from God that they worked hard over a lifetime to develop. The ability to communicate and work with the spirit world was a rare talent, given by God rather than achieved through ceremonies of initiation.

The Santeria religion also performs animal sacrifices, something that Mesa Blanca Espiritismo is adamantly against, often citing that Jesus was the last blood sacrifice needed. In Mesa Blanca, the use of blood in rituals was seen as practicing black magic and working with impure, less-evolved spirits. This they found both unnecessary and unacceptable. They also rejected the idea of a hierarchical priesthood based on ceremonies performed rather than on degrees of personal development. In fact, many *espiritistas* saw these practices as an easy way to defraud people.

NEW FORMS ARISE

As *espiritistas* incorporated Santeria or the 21 Divisions into their practices—some to a greater and some to a lesser degree—new forms of Espiritismo arose. These new forms sometimes incorporated initiation rituals, but not animal sacrifice. New ceremonies to work with *orishas* and *misterios* appeared that blended elements of both. Those following these new forms did their rituals totally in Spanish, leaving behind the original languages, and tended to focus on the major spirits of these traditions, ignoring other more minor spirits.

Unlike Mesa Blanca, which recognizes no hierarchy, these newer forms initiated priests and priestesses. They also formed lineages, meaning that the tradition was passed down via initiation from one person to another. One such variant is Santerismo, which blends Cuban Santeria with Espiritismo. In this form, the *orishas*, or divine beings of Santeria, are worked with alongside the guides of Mesa Blanca, thus creating a new type of *espiritista*, the *santerista*, who blended the music, rituals, and practices of the two traditions. Since Espiritismo is adamantly against animal sacrifice, *santeristas* do not practice it.

Sanse is another traditional practice formed in the late 1920s from the blend of Mesa Blanca and the 21 Divisions. As with Santerismo, certain elements of the 21 Divisions are used while others are left out. In Sanse, the *misterios* of the 21 Divisions become the major focus of the *protecciones* with which *espiritistas* work and new initiation rituals blending practices from both appear. These hybrid practices have their supporters as well as their detractors, who can be found among both traditional Puerto Rican *espiritistas* and Cuban *santeros*. Many *santeros* consider them to be disrespectful of their tradition, their history, and the *orishas*. To add to the confusion, many *santeristas* identify themselves as *santeros*. And for many traditional *espiritistas*, these newer forms simply contradict the basic tenets of their faith.

CLEANSE THE SPIRIT—THEN EAT

Shaking like a leaf gently rustling in the wind, Doña Juana sat with Joanna at the dining room table. As shivers gently rose and fell down her body, she waved her hands in the air as if rubbing an invisible glass wall around her. Her voice suddenly became hoarse and harsh, and she began to speak with a thick accent.

"*Irabansiabalantabansai* . . . That mother-in-law of yours wants to make your life miserable. She puts the kids in a bad way. When they are with you, they don't listen or obey you. And she tears into the ear of your husband too."

La madama, a spirit of cleansing and wisdom, had taken over Doña Juana's body and was speaking through her. She continued telling Joanna the reason why she was seated before her, explaining how, little by little, problems had arisen in her relationships and her home. Her mother-in-law was too *pendiente*, or watchful, of every little thing going on. Being watched in this way was obviously not a good thing (see chapter 10).

"*Te vamos limpiar, vamos limpiar esa casa* (We are going to clean you and clean that house)," Doña Juana said. "Then I am going to send in the Indians to watch and guard you." Then she stood up and raised Joanna to her feet, gripping her with such strength and force that she shook her. As she did so, she began speaking again.

"*Irabansiabalantabansai, limpiandote, purificandote.* Cleansing you, purifying you, getting rid of this negative energy on you, clearing you, with the light of God, the force of *la madama. Irabansiabalantabansai.*"

As she prayed, she began to pass her trembling hands just inches from Joanna's body, grabbing an invisible material as she passed over, which she dropped into a large bowl of water sitting on the table. She did this over and over while she prayed and talked, almost yelling at times. After rubbing her hands briskly with Florida Water to remove negativity from them, she grabbed Joanna's hands, lifting them as high as she could.

"*Con los Indios te vas, y con los Indios tu vienes, para traerte proteccion suerte y todos los bienes* (With the Indians you go and with the Indians you come, to bring you protection, luck, and all good things)," she said, jerking Joanna's hands down with a mighty force and letting go. Then she clapped a few times and a slight tremor seemed to pass through Joanna's body. Dizzy and slightly euphoric, she clutched at the edge of the table to regain her footing.

Doña Juana then went to the kitchen and removed the lid from a huge pot of steaming rice. Turning to Joanna, she said: "*Ya lista pa comer* (Ready to eat)?" Joanna sat down, gathering herself as she nodded.

Doña Juana had literally gathered up all the negative energy that was causing Joanna to be covered in a dark cloud. She had scraped away the negativity that had been piling up on her crusty layer by crusty layer. Once cleansed (and fed), Joanna started to experience greater peace, healing, and clarity in her life.

Chapter 3

THE WAR AGAINST MESA BLANCA

To differentiate his form of Spiritism from more traditional forms, Allen Kardec characterized it as Scientific Spiritism. Kardecists focused on philosophy and considered Spiritism to be a type of science rather than a religion. Their intention was to bring about social change and encourage enlightenment, understanding, purpose, and progressive consciousness. They rejected many of the practices of traditional *espiritistas*, including the use of altars and working with the spirits for change, healing, and divination. They were adamantly against all things that they considered "superstitions" and the teachings of "less-evolved people."

So it is not surprising that the Kardecists very quickly started a campaign against Mesa Blanca Espiritismo. They wanted to differentiate themselves from *espiritistas* whose practices they considered backward, barbaric, and unevolved. They wrote and published articles against Mesa Blanca, claiming that Mesa Blanca *espiritistas* were charlatans. They even coined a new and derogatory name for them, referring to them as *espiriteros*, which was clearly intended as a slur. They also mocked and ridiculed those who practiced or believed in

Mesa Blanca, making fun of them for referring to practitioners as *medicos* (doctors), even though it was the *espiritistas* who provided most of the healing needed by most of the population.

The introduction of the American influence on the island helped the growth of Scientific Spiritism, but it also encouraged efforts—although at first gently—to rid the native population of their traditional practices. With the Americans came the Protestants, who sought to grow their religious mission in Puerto Rico. At first, much like the Catholics, they didn't seem to have much of a problem with the Kardecists. Instead, they joined them in their efforts to get rid of the Mesa Blanca *espiritistas*.

At the end of the 1940s, after World War II, a formal campaign of modernization and Americanization began in Puerto Rico. New programs were instituted to modernize the island and its rural populations, which had suffered great economic and political damage because of America's wartime activities. The new programs offered better housing, education, and health services to the majority of the population. But they also started a full-scale battle against traditional beliefs and healing practices. The government launched an open attack on *brujeria* and Popular Espiritismo that was backed by both the educational and the medical systems. This attack was headed mainly by the upper-class elite, including the Kardecists.

Now financially backed by the Protestants and the Americans, the Kardecists had ample resources to continue their war against Mesa Blanca Espiritismo and all those who followed its tenets. They used the media to support their cause to eradicate these "barbaric" practices from the island, veiling their campaign of destruction in platitudes about the need to "educate" the lower classes about their "superstitions."

Mockery, ridicule, and defamation of *espiritistas*, *brujos*, *curanderos*, and all those who followed them became regular features in the

ESPIRITISMO

newspapers, which portrayed all adherents of Mesa Blanca as stupid and "unevolved." Various mini-campaigns were launched to defame as many *curanderos*, *brujos*, *espiritistas*, and professional mediums as possible.

While the Kardecists waged their savage war on Mesa Blanca, the Protestant and Evangelical branches of Christianity started their own growth campaigns. In fact, they began growing on the island like a raging fire. Unlike the Kardecists, who focused on ridiculing "an unevolved people," the churches focused on converting and saving souls and literally demonizing Mesa Blanca and *brujeria*. This caused divisions in many families and households that followed several different spiritual paths. In fact, it was not uncommon for the father of a household to be a Pentecostal Christian, the mother to be an *espiritista*, and the grandmother to be a traditional Catholic. In such households, children inevitably grew up with mixed beliefs.

Nevertheless, despite these campaigns, many Puerto Rican *espiritistas* became famous for their healing and spiritual abilities. One of the most famous of these was known as *La Samaritana*, the Good Samaritan. This talented healer drew tens of thousands to her healing sessions, at which she channeled several spirits. During her long career, she was featured in newspapers and magazines, and on the radio. Although the Kardecists tried their best, they were of course unable to bring her down. The miracles spoke for themselves.

Another famous *espiritista* was Doña Conchita, who regularly drew large crowds to her spiritual center, where they received treatment with spiritual injections of the universal fluid. After waving her hands over people a few times, she touched an arm or an affected area with her index finger, which acted as the "needle" through which she channeled the essential fluid through her own body and directed it into her patients. Some reports claimed that a mark often appeared in the exact place where she had placed her finger, making it look as if the person had received an injection.

These eradication campaigns lasted for almost forty years, stopping only in the early 1980s. Over the course of time, however, the Protestants as well as the Americans removed their financial backing of the Kardecists. Moreover, the Protestants not only removed their financial backing; they also began to denounce all forms of Espiritismo, including Scientific Spiritism, considering all such practices to be demonic. As a result, Kardecist centers suffered a huge loss of membership. Of the many huge spiritual centers that had flourished on the island, very few survived.

LOST ROOTS

Immediately after I published my first book, *The 21 Divisions: Mysteries and Magic of Dominican Voodoo* (Weiser Books, 2020), people began to flood me with email begging me to write a book about Espiritismo. They had come to the same realization that I had so many years ago—that Mesa Blanca Espiritismo was slowly fading away, at least in its original form. It seems that Puerto Ricans were finally beginning to seek out and reconnect with their spiritual roots. They were looking for a way to get in touch with their own ancestral spiritual heritage. What they were looking for was, in fact, a way to reconnect with Mesa Blanca.

You would think that this would be easy—especially in the world of connectivity and information that we live in today. But nothing could be farther from the truth. Unfortunately, because of the success of the war against Espiritismo, finding a Mesa Blanca spiritual center where true Puerto Rican Espiritismo is practiced has become like looking for water in the desert. The eradication campaign against Mesa Blanca was so effective that even those who practice it or identify themselves with its principles have ended up being ambivalent about it and only speak about it in hushed tones.

Even families who once followed the path won't speak of Espiritismo and act as if it never existed. Those searching for their roots have thus been denied access to them, and have had no choice but to begin looking elsewhere. As a result, many of them have turned to Santeria because, over time, it has become easier to find a *santero* or *santera* on the island than to find a Mesa Blanca *espiritista*. As Santeria began to replace Mesa Blanca, more and more Puerto Ricans began walking the Santeria path, and this means following and practicing Cuban, rather than Puerto Rican, Espiritismo. This, in turn, has led to fewer and fewer apprentices wanting to study and commit to the Mesa Blanca path. As a result, although there are still rituals and *reuniones* being done on the island today, in most cases these are performed as part of one of these other paths. It has become increasingly difficult to find survivals of pure Puerto Rican Espiritismo.

REVIVAL

In the late 1980s, however, a movement began to save the culture and identity of the Puerto Rican people. This sparked great interest in the traditional healing practices and herbalism of the island, which were promoted more as holistic and herbal healing techniques. *Espiritistas* thus morphed from being "superstitious backward charlatans" to being "keepers of herbal knowledge and wisdom." In the age of environmentalism, this made them cultural icons.

By the 1980s, medical science had "discovered" that many of the herbal and traditional treatments given by *espiritistas* were actually effective in curing illness. In some cases, they were even more effective than mainstream medicine. As they learned more and more about how human beings worked, the medical establishment also started to become aware of the *espiritistas'* natural role as psychiatrists who helped people solve problems and resolve pressing issues in their lives.

Since the late 1990s, there has been a huge revival of cultural pride among Puerto Ricans. In fact, in the new millenium, many terms like *espiritista*, *brujo*, and *curandero* are no longer ridiculed, but are rather used to express a type of ancestral pride. It has even become normal to see reports about the wisdom or healing powers of *espiritistas* on Spanish-language newscasts.

Among the older generation who were indoctrinated for so long against Espiritismo, however, this change has not come easily. Many of these older people continue to speak of Espiritismo in hushed tones. Even more continue to reject the practices of Espiritismo out of hand, even if they were raised in the tradition. And yet more tend to treat their cultural heritage like a bad secret that needs to be hidden away forever.

Unfortunately, today's efforts at revival don't appear to be pursued as vigorously as the campaign against Espiritismo was. In fact, the campaign against Espiritismo was so effective in wiping out Puerto Rico's cultural identity and spiritual traditions that the revival has barely scratched the surface of the damage already done. Despite feeble attempts to re-empower Espiritismo and *espiritistas*, Mesa Blanca continues to fade away.

A SHATTERED PAST

I walked closely behind them along a windy, narrow abandoned trail that looked as if no one had used it in many years. Tia Berta led the way with a big knife to cut away the brush; Tia Nereida trailed a few feet behind me.

"Where are we going?" I asked, curious to know.

"You'll see when we get there," Tia Nereida responded hastily.

After walking for a good fifteen minutes through a field and lots of overgrown and out-of-control shrubbery, we arrived at what appeared to be an old, abandoned shack made of wooden planks. It looked as if it were falling apart, as nature had already taken up residence all over and around it, growing all types of green grasses and plants through cracks in the planks.

Tia Nereida whacked some greenery here and there so that we could push our way through what had once been a doorway with an actual door but was now just an opening covered with a plank of wood. Inside, the sun was beaming through all the cracks in the walls, just enough so that we could see clearly.

On one side of the small space, a tree appeared to be growing out of the wall. Its trunk and roots were inside the structure, but it had made its way through the wall in search of sunlight. Various other life forms had also made their home in the shack since its abandonment. There were little lizards running around and plenty of bugs.

Across from where we entered stood a wooden table, dirty and falling apart. It leaned to one side, as one leg had apparently been broken off and was shorter than the others. A bit of broken glass lay on it, along with a few other objects. The head of a statue of St. Claire that appeared to have broken off—or been deliberately removed—sat among the rubble. The rest of her body lay on a long table that stood behind the lopsided one.

"This is your family," Tia Nereida said, emphasizing the words *your family*. As she spoke, she waved her hand around and gazed in all directions. Then, taking a lighter out of her pocket, she drew a cigar that she had been holding to her lips and lit it. Puffing gently, she let out clouds of smoke that surrounded her.

With just those few words, she had spoken volumes. Indeed, my family *was* broken, its traditions destroyed. Once united under the banner of Espiritismo, they had shattered into fragments—very much like that broken statue in that broken-down shack we were in. Each group had become like a little island, succumbing to what many other Puerto Rican families succumbed to—modernization, Americanization, Christianization, and secularization.

Christianity had done the worst damage. Because of the highly spiritual and religious upbringing of most of my elders, once they were converted to Christianity, it became the most important guiding force for them. This conversion created a tension that forced them to choose between family and God.

"This place is like this because of some of my brothers and sisters," Nereida said, gazing at me intently. "The Christian ones." She was telling me that this little "shack" had been broken down by vandals who wanted to "cleanse" my family of its religious beliefs. They wanted to "destroy the devil" in my family and chose to do so by destroying this place.

Because this place was not just a shack. At one time, it had been a well-established spiritual healing center that was continually alive with people coming from various parts of the island to receive spiritual help. Here, bi-monthly group rituals had taken place in which messages were communicated to people from the spirit world.

"This spiritual center was built by my father for my mother, after the one that she had before fell apart," said Tia Berta. "He built it right over top of the old one," she marveled, pointing at the ground beneath her.

"I have so many fond memories of this place," Tia Berta continued. "As a child, my siblings and I used to play in these woods while my mother worked inside. My sisters and I helped to take care of the center when we came of an age to do so. Really, we spent just as much time here as we did at home, because this is where Mama was.

"This center was regularly active until my mother became too old to work here. We used to hold *sessiones* (rituals), do healings, and help the sick. Anyone who didn't have work or didn't have enough to eat could come here and be fed." Her face beamed with fondness for the memories of the miracles that had taken place there.

Once Tia Berta's mother—my great-grandmother—was too old to do spiritual work, she moved to the US mainland, where there were relatives to care for her. The property fell into the hands of her two eldest sons, who had both become Pentecostal Christians. And they weren't alone. Many islanders had become either Pentecostal or Evangelical Christians, and they all seemed to feel that it was their duty to "save the family from devil worship." So the spiritual center, which had been a place of healing, elevation, and beauty for many people over many decades, was vandalized again and again.

My aunts and I stayed for a little while longer, but the sun began to go down. After a few deep sighs, Tia Berta said: "Let's go." We left the dilapidated shack, the abandoned spiritual center, and made our way back to the house.

Chapter 4

EL MUNDO ESPIRITUAL—THE WORLD OF SPIRIT

Espiritistas believe in one God, seen as the beginning and the end, the ultimate and eternal One, an infinite intelligence. In the beginning, only God existed, as the primary cause of all things. In Spanish, the word for God is *Dios*, and *espiritistas* often call him *Papa Dios*, or Father God.

In the world of Espiritismo, God created all of existence using *la luz*, the light, which contains two principle elements—spirit and matter. The element of spirit consists of consciousness; the element of matter consists of energy.

La luz (plural, *luces*) is one of the most important terms used in Espiritismo. On one level, it speaks of the pure universal fluid that ties all of existence together (see below). It is power, or *fuerza*, in its purest and most raw form. Everything in existence has this power, which, in many shamanic traditions, is called life force. This *fuerza* is the very power that causes life to be. As *espiritistas* say: *Cada quien nace con su luz*. Everyone is born with their light.

The *espiritisma's* view of God's creation consists of several characteristic elements: planes of existence that interact, a universal element that binds all creation together (the universal fluid), reincarnation and development, magnetic emissions called *corrientes,* and an entire pantheon of spirits.

PLANES OF EXISTENCE

Within creation, God created many realms or planes of existence, layered one upon the other like slides in a projector. The totality of these planes forms the universe as a whole. Just as with a projector, the various colors and images on the slides, although separated by a thin layer, affect each other and change what we perceive and how we perceive it.

Before creating *el mundo*, the physical world, God created various spiritual planes as well, populating them with spirits. The spirits who live in these spiritual realms are disincarnate, meaning they do not possess bodies. These spiritual planes are invisible to the naked eye. On the physical plane of existence, the material elements of the universal fluid manifest as objects, people, places, and animals. These physical entities then become vessels for Spirit, or the intelligent element. Spirits living on the physical plane—people and animals— have bodies and are incarnate.

All these levels coexist, layered one upon the other, and progress simultaneously. However, just as the eye cannot see all colors, so not all spirits are aware of all other spirits on other planes of existence. For instance, spirits cannot always see people, and vice versa. Just think of how, before the microscope was invented, many tiny beings like amoebas existed that were totally unknown to humans.

UNIVERSAL FLUID

The universal fluid acts as a magnetic force that binds everything together. It acts as a glue that ties together everything that matches energetically. It also causes the two elements within the light to act upon each other. The universal fluid thus provides the active tension and friction of the universe that maintains it in existence.

The universal fluid is also known as the magnetic fluid, or the vital fluid. It is absorbent and takes on the properties of the spirits and matter that it encompasses. Each of these elements shifts the universal fluid, coloring it with its own nature.

REINCARNATION

All spirits are undergoing a constant process of development, whether they are aware of it or not. This is because the purpose of every soul is to develop spiritually. Just as your body develops throughout the course of your life, so does your spirit. Unlike your physical body, however, which will eventually dissipate, your spiritual body will continue to pass from one existence to another.

All spirits start at the same place, then grow and renew themselves through a process of many lives and rebirths. This is called reincarnation. As an individual spirit develops, its light and power grow. Thus all of us have the innate capacity to connect with God and the Divine, because we are all spirits inhabiting bodies.

Each of the spiritual realms helps to develop the spirits within that realm. As one of the realms, Earth serves as one of many classrooms for individual spirits. In fact, each spirit is on a journey back toward God—a great journey whose purpose is to reunite with God, to return to the oneness of the Great Spirit where the individual spirit becomes free of all chains and bonds.

As with all journeys, there are various stages in this process. What helps us progress on this journey is reincarnation, which occurs, not only in the physical realm, but also within the spiritual realms of existence. In Espiritismo, reincarnation is always progressive.

Every spirit has personal will, to a greater or lesser degree. However, this is not *free* will. The amount of free will each spirit has is determined by how much purity that spirit has attained. Spirits with lesser degrees of free will must submit to those who have attained a greater degree.

MAGNETIC EMISSIONS

Since everything is made of light, everything radiates light outward. When this light radiates outward, it takes on the qualities and properties of the vessel through which it passes. Thus it is no longer in its original pure state, but has become individualized. These emissions of light are known as *fluidos* or *corrientes,* fluids or currents. Currents that come via the spirits are known as spiritual currents. Currents that come from objects, people, and animals are known as psychic currents.

The properties of these *corrientes* are dependent on the actions, manner of being, and perceptions of the spirit emitting the light. Because they are made up of the universal fluid, which takes on the properties of whatever it encompasses, they take on the qualities of the thoughts, emotions, and energies they carry. There are many ways that these qualities are expressed in Espiritismo. The light can be beautiful, dim, bright, strong, weak, or dark.

The energy emitted in these currents creates a magnetic force field known as the aura (see chapter 10). The aura acts like a magnet that attracts energies and spirits that are like itself, and concurrently repels energies that are opposite to it. Since an individual's aura is made up of that person's currents, the aura has a base level, but also contains various levels that are continually changing and that are affected by the state of being of the spirit to whom it belongs.

INTERACTION AND COMMUNICATION

Since all realms essentially exist at the same time and place, spirits and humans constantly affect one another, whether they realize it or not. All beings are affected by energy currents, seen or unseen, and they, in turn, affect the currents. Whenever you feel "bad vibes" or "good vibes"—or any kind of energy for that matter—what you are feeling are these currents. And just as the eyes can not perceive all colors, so some currents can be perceived while others cannot.

Since we are all spirits, we can and do communicate regularly with other spirits. For the vast majority, this happens unconsciously, but we are all born with spiritual senses, just as we are born with physical senses. It's just that most people have not developed these senses enough to be aware of the actions of the spirits around them.

The qualities of a spirit's *corrientes*, and therefore its aura, exert a magnetic attraction toward those beings who share its qualities. Clean clear currents thus attract clean, clear, and pure spirits. Dark lights attract impure spirits. Each person's currents attract spirits who share the same nature or energy as that person's aura.

Spirits can and do affect and communicate with each other using their vital fluids, or currents. This occurs through three types of magnetic influence that are directed by one being, called the magnetizer, toward another, called the target:

- *Spiritual magnetism.* This is the influence the spirits exert directly, without the use of a human channel. This happens whenever there is a good connection or a negative attachment. Through spiritual magnetism, spirits can influence, direct, and affect thoughts and feelings, and therefore actions. They can suggest ideas, both positive and negative. Since their energy is more ethereal, it is easier for spirits to work in this way than to manipulate the physical realm. This is, in fact, the most common way they operate.

- *Human magnetism.* This occurs when magnetizers are living people who can direct their own currents to influence others—for good or for ill. People are born with varying degrees of magnetism and they have the power to use it.

- *Mediumistic magnetism.* This form of magnetism operates when a spirit's fluids are directed through a human channel, merging and mixing the currents. This is the strongest of the three types. We are all used in this way to some degree, whether we are aware of it or not.

Magnetic influence is a two-way street, however. We can also affect the spiritual world and the spirits themselves. By taking certain actions, living in certain ways, and being certain kinds of people, we affect our own currents and auras, as well as the spirits and the nature of the spirits that surround us. Thus we participate in a loop of interaction and communication with the spiritual world.

SPIRIT REALMS

There are good spirits and bad spirits, and the nature of each spirit determines its place in the spiritual world. There are three realms in this world, two of which are further subdivided.

Good spirits are also known as *espiritus de luz,* or spirits of light. But in addition to being a spirit of light, a spirit can also *traer una luz,* or bring a light. In this case, the spirit brings forward a revelation or another faculty. Good spirits choose to help lesser spirits evolve.

Impure spirits are called *luces oscuras,* or dark or negative lights. These spirits act as parasites to the light. Like black holes, they take and take, but never give back. Whereas spirits of light bring blessings and help lesser spirits evolve, spirits of darkness eat up blessings and work to draw higher spirits down, causing a backward motion. By doing so, they feed off the pain they've created—sort of like crabs in a barrel.

But the light is non-discriminating. Its *fuerza,* its power, is not the same as its purity. A spirit can have a strong light whether it uses it for positive or negative ends. Thus, on all planes, there are spirits who are powerful, although they may not all be good spirits.

Pure Spirits

Pure spirits are the closest to God and most closely embody the pure principles of the spiritual world. They are also known as the perfect spirits, or the superior spirits. All pure spirits have reached a state of total enlightenment. As enlightened beings, they have been absorbed into God and act only on God's will.

Within this realm, there are no levels or degrees. Nor do these spirits have names. Rather, they work on behalf of principles and pure energies. Spirits of truth and love, spirits of compassion, and certain angels, cherubim, and seraphim are all considered to be pure spirits as well.

When the pure spirits come through, their wisdom helps lead to awakening, clarity, and wisdom. Many of them are teachers, spiritual masters, or master teachers. They dispense the pure teachings of truth, inspire epiphanies, and show the way.

Good Spirits

Good spirits are aware of God and have some understanding of the Divine. They seek to do good in the world, and to be charitable, kind, and loving toward others. They work consciously on their own development and progression. Within this realm, there are many types of spirits that have various levels of light.

This realm is home to the spiritual guides and *protecciones,* or protectors. This level also includes the good and elevated ancestors, the dead, patron saints, and guardian spirits. Much of an *espiritista's* work is to develop relationships with and connections to this level of spirits.

Impure Spirits

Impure spirits are those most attached to the material world and material things. In fact, they are enwrapped within them. They do not know or understand God. Therefore, many of them seek material and physical pleasures.

Because they are attached closely to the material plane, these spirits are incredibly powerful and talented in controlling things on the physical planes. They can and will use this power to manipulate people into situations that will only further their suffering. Some of these spirits are just mischievous for no reason, while others like to create physical phenomena just to scare people—like moving objects physically.

Many impure spirits are parasitic in nature. They seek to attach themselves to a good host and slowly drain its energy. They cause blockages, confusion, and suffering. In Espiritismo, these spirits are often the source of illnesses that people suffer on mental, emotional, and physical levels.

These spirits are naturally attracted to suffering and the various evils that help produce it. Often, they encourage evil actions just to cause pain. Whenever there is a release of negativity, it attracts impure spirits, who feed on the situation and pain it has caused. If the suffering continues for a long period of time, these spirits can even attach themselves to the person involved.

There are several groups of spirits within this realm. Here are just a few:

- *Espiritus atrasados* (set-back spirits) are arrested in their development and stuck at a certain point on their journey. They are either unwilling or unable to learn their lessons, resolve their karma, and move forward. They may also be repaying a karmic debt. Many of these spirits are not bad *per se*. But they are not necessarily good either. They tend to waste time, and to be ignorant and generally selfish. They often cause others harm through their own selfishness without necessarily intending to do so. They can be both compassionate and cruel. Among this group we find ghosts—spirits who are stuck in the physical realm, usually unwillingly—and poltergeists—spirits who like to cause disturbances in the physical realm, for instance by making loud noises or moving things around. We also find intranquil spirits here—spirits who are living in pain or who died in suffering and exist in a state remarkably like purgatory—as well as negative spirits with truly harmful intent—criminalistic, sociopathic, and psychopathic beings who lack remorse for their actions. Many of these spirits purposely seek to cause others suffering—not because the suffering of others lessens their own pain, but rather because they just enjoy watching others suffer.

- *Guias falsos* (false guides) are more powerful and dangerous than the *espiritus atrasados*. They seek to give improper guidance and to get people on the wrong path. Many of these spirits are strongly committed to their malicious task.

- *Demonios* (demons) are even more sinister than the false guides. *Espiritistas* see demons in the same way that Christians do—as spirits who were once angels who decided to go against God. Because they were once angels, they are incredibly powerful. Many of them inspire greed, lust, false pride, envy, jealousy, and many of the other negative traits to which we humans are prone. Although these spirits are impure, however, that doesn't mean that they are ignorant. In fact, many of them are highly intelligent and informed about the world, because they are the spirits most confined to the material plane, with all its joys and its sorrows. Many demons are ancient and have been in the realm of impure spirits for an exceedingly long time. Thus, they know about the past and about how people act, and they use this knowledge to manipulate others, including those who can communicate with the spiritual world. They do this by mixing truth and lies in order to create trust. In Puerto Rico, we have a proverb: The devil knows more because he's old than because he's the devil.

PAYING TUPATE

Tupate was Titi Berta's main spiritual guide. According to Berta, he was a Taino Indian who had been a spiritual leader and shaman in his tribe. He was wise, kind, protective, and a great healer, and Berta referred to him as "my Indian of peace." Tupate was easily pleased and attended to, she said.

Although her mother and sisters were all mediums, Berta was always very scared of the spirits. When Tupate revealed himself to her in a dream after she had found a *cemi* stone in the woods (see chapter 6), she said: "I tried to put it out of my mind as much as possible. I did not want to see ghosts or anything. Much less deal with the dead! I told them they had got the wrong girl."

In the dream, Berta saw a huge Indian sitting beside her. "He had a white feather on his head," she remembered. "He didn't say anything, but I felt as if I were seeing an old friend. Then I heard someone calling my name. I didn't have another dream of him until months later. It was the same dream, but this time he waved at me. Then he pointed to my stomach.

"A few days later I had the worst pain in my stomach—like someone was trying to rip it out of my body. My mother prepared teas and gave me remedies, but they didn't work. She said that this wasn't physical; it was spiritual. I would have to attend her next *velada* so we could get to the bottom of it.

"During the *velada*, one of the mediums said: 'You're paying for your faculties. That Indian with the white feathers sent you a sign. Now you're paying for not listening. That's what's wrong in your stomach.'

"I was told the illness would pass when the time was up, but that I had to pay my dues, as every medium must. There was no quick fix for this one. In the meantime, I was told to display the three virtues as much as possible—faith, hope, and charity. The medium then rubbed my body with oils and prayed for me.

"Although this was not what I wanted to hear, what could I do? Nothing but have faith in my mother's abilities and the team of mediums that would instruct me in *la Obra*.

"I was sick for almost another month—some days more, some days less. Some days I could barely get out of bed. But I kept my faith and hoped that I would return to normal. I prayed day in and day out. Some days, I did not feel that I was accomplishing anything by praying and I just wanted to give up. But every day at least twice I prayed. I talked to the Indian and prayed for his spirit too.

"Then one night, the Indian came again in a dream. I was lying on a large stone slab with a pile of stones on my stomach. The Indian started removing them one by one, and they changed into lights in his hand. He took these lights and shoved them in different areas of my body. By the end of the dream, there were only three small stones left on my stomach. I woke up.

"That day, I felt better than I had felt in months. I remember it very clearly. I woke up full of life, feeling 90 percent better. My mother was so happy to see me happy that she made me a huge breakfast. And I ate it all. When I lifted my head from my plate, I saw the head of the Indian on the wall looking at me. It shocked me and I ran from the room. When my mother came to see what was wrong, I told her, but she just started laughing at me. That was the joke of the family for the next week.

"With each day, I felt better and better. I was told that I would have to give a *velada* to this Indian. So my mother gave me a list of things I needed to get. Among them were flowers, herbs, rum, cigars, and, most important, something to represent my Indian.

"When the night came for the *velada*, the mediums and my mother gave me a spiritual bath and I dressed in a white top and skirt. Then I was put in a chair facing the mediums. At the end of the table were all the flowers and herbs and other items I had been told to bring, arranged in a circle around the object that represented my Indian—the stone I had found that had triggered my initial dream. I didn't really know what it was, but that night I would find out.

"The mediums started the prayers, then my mother stood and began a long prayer inviting my Indian to come give and receive. After this prayer, the mediums started relating their visions to me. My Indian smoked a cigar. He was always sitting. His favorite colors were white and light yellow. He was a healer. Whenever I felt a presence in my room as a child, he was there. He was an Indian of peace. And they said I had something that belonged to him.

"As I was told all these things, I occasionally felt the fluids near me or touching me. At one point, as I was feeling this on my right side, a medium confirmed it by telling me the Indian was touching my right arm at that moment.

"Later, one of the mediums came to tell me that the stone I had found in the woods belonged to the Indian. It was his home and I must take care of it."

Chapter 5

EL CUADRO ESPIRITUAL— THE SPIRITUAL FRAME

Espiritistas believe that we are all born with what is known as a *cuadro espiritual*, or spiritual frame, that constitutes our spiritual power. The process of life actively influences and changes this frame and, with each lifetime, it is developed more and more. This frame contains our spiritual abilities, our guardian angels, our spiritual guides, and our karma. It acts as a vessel, a home, and a tool for the spirits. Like *la luz*, it can have various properties—light or dark, dull or bright, strong or weak.

Some of the spirits of the *cuadro* are born with us and will form the foundation of our lives—just as we are all born into families. But many other spirits will be attracted to us throughout life. They may become a permanent part of our *cuadro,* or they may simply be visitors throughout the course of life. Many spirits may also connect with us because of their likeness to or sympathy for us.

Spirits use the *cuadro* to work with people, and to influence and communicate with them. They also use it to work *through* them. Many people confuse their spiritual frame with the spirits that are within it. But the spiritual frame is more like the house in which the spirits live and work. They use it as a tool and as a vessel for their powers.

In fact, the *cuadro* can also act independently. It has its own powers and abilities. It often acts on our behalf, doing work without us even being aware or asking or trying to direct it. In this way, it can bring blessings or it can wreak havoc in our lives. Thus it affects us at a core level, and reveals how connected we are to our path and our purpose in this life.

Our *cuadros* dictate how we experience life as well as our purpose and our life lessons. The practices of Espiritismo are designed to grow and evolve the light consciously. When we do this, our lives and our paths become *bendecida,* or blessed. This manifests itself as good luck, material blessings, and various spiritual abilities. By empowering certain aspects of the *cuadro,* we can bring balance and progress on our path.

SPIRITS OF THE CUADRO

Some of the spirits of the *cuadro* are born with us; they have been there since birth. Moreover, they may have come with us from previous lifetimes.

We are all born with a guardian angel, a patron saint, a principal guide, ancestors, and causal spirits. Each of these spirits performs a function for us and has since the very beginning of our lives. As we begin to live, spirits who are attracted to us by likeness and sympathy will also attach themselves to us. It is not important to know the names of all your spiritual guides, or to work with them all. Some of them will be there only temporarily or during certain phases and then leave, whereas others may become a permanent part of your *cuadro*.

Angeles Custodios (Guardian Angels)

We are all born with a holy guardian angel, given to us by God to watch over us and act as the personal voice of God for us. This spirit is of the highest importance. It is one of the pure spirits, and stays with us throughout the course of our entire lifetime.

Guardian angels work to protect and guide individuals toward their highest good. They are never given a name or characteristics, however. As beings of pure light, they have no traits of their own, although we may each have different experiences and each perceive our guardian angels in different ways. Before *espiritistas* do any work, they always ask for the permission of the guardian angel and request that their passage be allowed. Without this, the light cannot flow through and empower the *cuadro* to do its work.

Espiritistas honor these spirits on October 2nd—the feast of all guardian angels—giving them white candles, sweets, and clear glasses of water. *Espiritistas* also pray to their own guardian angels, always seeking their guidance and blessing before doing any work. Unlike any other spirit, guardian angels have no personal will; they rather express the will of the Divine for the individual.

Guias Principales (Principal Guides)

Guias principales, or principal spiritual guides, are born with us as well, and their job is to guide and help us on our life's journey—and, if we so choose, on our spiritual journey. Coming from the realm of the good spirits, these guides help us develop greater light and increase our capacity to grow closer to God.

Of all the spiritual guides that *espiritistas* work with, *guias principales* are the most important, as they direct all the activity of the *cuadro*. They are usually identified through a long process of investigative rituals and confirmatory experiences. We often share many of the attributes of this guide, which strongly influences our personality, our lifestyle, and our path.

Espiritistas sometimes refer to this guide as *mi muerto* or *tu muerto*, my dead or your dead. This terminology is not to be confused with *los muertos*, or the dead, however, with which many *espiritistas* also work (see chapter 9). Principal guides don't pertain to the realm of the dead any longer and cannot be any living person we have known in the course of our lifetime, since they are born with us.

Espiritistas work at *desarrollando*—deepening their connection with the principal guide, which works only with the individual *espiritista*. This is an exclusive relationship. This guide cannot be called upon by any other individual. It simply will not respond unless the *espiritista* is working for that individual. This guide is often the one who speaks on behalf of, or as an intermediary for, the other spirits in the *cuadro*, coming through *en corriente*, or via the currents.

Patrones (Patron Saints)

The patron saint is a major force in our spiritual frame—one that shields us from harm. This *entidad*, or entity, provides a huge overarching current within our lives, its underlying energy influencing everything we do and become. Its identity is usually revealed during investigations with an elder *espiritista*. Although called patron saints, these spirits aren't necessarily Catholic saints. They could be Hindu or Buddhist deities, spirits from another tradition, *orishas*, or *misterios*.

Our patron saints are like parents to us. Unlike guardian angels, they usually have well-known likes, dislikes, and associations. Unlike both guardian angels and principal guides, they are usually connected to many individuals and are not exclusive to just one. They exist on the level of *protecciones*, or protections, but the level at which we interact, communicate, and work with them depends on our level of development.

Los Difuntos (Ancestors)

Our ancestors are known as *los difuntos*. Ancestral work is foundational in Espiritismo, as our ancestors are intrinsically linked to us and our ancestral lineage provides us with so much of who we are. Our DNA, many of our traits and characteristics, and the things with which we identify or stand against all come down through our ancestral line.

No family line is without its karma, however, without its chains that tie it to the past. We all stand on the backs of our ancestors, as we say; they are the reason for our being here. Thus we all enter the world with some ancestral karma that can create negative cycles in the lives of those who are connected to it. It is up to us to break out of these cycles. Thus ancestral healing is essential to us all.

Ancestral karma is usually what lies behind family curses. Negative karma will continue to play itself out in a family line until the cycle is broken. But this often doesn't happen, simply because no one wants to take responsibility for the negative energies and work on them directly. And even when individuals do make the effort, they often end up saving only themselves. It may be too late for others who have already begun on the cycle.

Ancestral work is done using many healing practices, one of which is ancestral elevation, which entails offering prayer, light, and water to *los difuntos*. By lighting a white candle for these spirits next to a glass of water, we give the spirit light and refreshment on its path.

Keeping an ancestral altar is another way to honor our past. This is a table, usually covered in white, that holds photos of passed loved ones and on which the ancestors are served by giving them light, attention, prayer, candles, water, and flowers. Some believe that everyone should keep an ancestral altar. This is not necessarily the case, however. For some, an ancestral altar may have adverse effects, especially in families that have suffered much trauma—which is not uncommon for those with a spiritual talent. For these individuals, other healing practices must occur before they can keep such an altar.

LAS CAUSAS

The negative spiritual energies held within the *cuadro* are known as *causas*. Just as we are born with good spirits in our spiritual frame, we are also born with certain negative entities that encourage our growth and development, and allow us to repay karma. These entities come from the realm of the impure spirits. As they are cleared, our capacity for interacting with good spirits develops and we become better protected against absorbing more negative spiritual baggage.

Since we all experience negativity throughout the course of our lives, we all end up with some connections to these negative spirits. The focus in Espiritismo is to heal these spirits and remove their attachments. *Espiritistas* work to be healed and free of these spirits and their forces so that they become empowered to help others in the same way. But those who have a strong light may use it for either positive or negative ends, so *espiritistas* must take care lest they fall prey to the impure spirits they work with and end up attracting more of them.

Espiritistas combat these negative energies with *la luz*, or light, which is also a term of response. During consultations and group rituals, the words *la luz* are said to confirm a *videncia,* an insight or vision that has been given. They assure that the message received is true, and may also be said as a way to give thanks or to confer blessings. As a result of various conditions, the light can be obstructed or contain dark patches or stains. *Espiritistas* are trained in various practices to unblock anything that may be obstructing the flow of their light. They also work to amplify their capacity to receive and channel the light purposefully. Novice *espiritistas* are often told by elders to *darle luz,* or to give light to either a spirit or to a *cuadro,* thus making it more powerful.

One such practice is to burn candles while praying. Novices practice this and other specific rituals to help them bring through greater light. The expression "put a light to such and such spirit" means to light a candle to the spirit for some specific purpose.

The spirits who come through the *cuadro* will be those who match the currents that are being emitted by the person in question. By extension, the *cuadro* itself becomes a reflection of the qualities of the light that flows.

ESPIRITISTAS

Espiritistas are people who know that the spiritual world exists and are willing to work with it. Either by virtue of heightened spiritual senses or through life experience, they have become aware of the presence and power of spirits and understand that there is an ongoing interaction between the spiritual and physical planes of existence.

Espiritistas strive to be channels for the principles of faith, hope, charity, and love. They do this through actions and deeds, not words. They are practitioners, not philosophers. It is not sufficient that their actions and words attest to their calling; their very being and character must reflect it.

Espiritistas are aware of the spiritual world and its power in the physical world. While others usually manifest the currents of the spiritual world unknowingly, *espiritistas* recognize them and work to become vessels for the manifestation of that which comes from the higher realms. This is what distinguishes them from the rest.

In order to be vessels and conduits for the higher realms, *espiritistas* must attend to their health in a holistic manner. They take care of their bodies as carefully as they take care of their spirits. They live healthy lifestyles in order to embody a clean and clear current. Their habits, diet, and exercise all contribute to their capacity to serve God and the spirits. They also make sure to attend to any physical health concerns quickly, because they know that they are responsible for the vessel they have been given.

Espiritistas also understand that every soul is working its way toward God, and they make a conscious effort to further that journey. They therefore explore every area of their own lives and accept responsibility for themselves. They understand that we all make mistakes on the path, but they try to minimize them and to give their best to their mission.

Those who work with the spirit world must be accountable for the currents that work through them. They must take responsibility for dealing with the fluids that are manifested and yet to manifest in their work. They must care for their auras, their *cuadros,* and their spiritual bodies. They must seek the guidance of the pure and good spirits and follow it. *Espiritistas* keep their promises and fulfill their commitments, always finishing what they have begun. And they always follow the divine will and purpose.

ESPIRITISTA EXTRAORDINAIRE

I had flown to Florida to consult with an *espiritista* who had agreed to let me use her altar to do my work. I was excited to meet her because it had been a long time since I had met someone who was a practitioner of Mesa Blanca Espiritismo.

Doña Ana was a short Puerto Rican woman of about sixty with short salt-and-pepper hair. When I arrived, she was wearing a pair of old blue jeans and a green blouse. We hit it off right away.

Ana led me to her finished basement, where she kept her altar. Half of the space was set up as a den and bar, with a large TV, a pool table, and a huge sectional sofa. The other half, hidden behind the wall opposite the stairs, housed the altar.

The altar room was gigantic. Floor-to-ceiling shelves lined all four walls, and all the shelves were crowded with statues of saints and guides, plaques, candles, and flowers. There were at least 300 statues, and more than fifty lit seven-day glass-encased candles. I didn't even bother to count how many dozens of flowers were lining the room. In the center was a huge old cherry-wood desk with a leather office chair behind it. In front stood two cozy armchairs for those who came for consultations.

I had arrived a day early to make sure that everything was in place for my work. Since I would be around all day, Ana invited me to spend time with her while she worked. She was kind enough to allow me to sit in her altar room and watch her interact with her clients. This is one of the most beautiful gifts an *espiritista* can give you. It requires a huge amount of trust, but allows you to learn a great deal.

Ana had three clients coming that day. The first to arrive was Carmelita, a tall woman of about sixty who had been coming to Doña Ana for several years. Having grown up around Espiritismo, she herself was an *espiritista*, but not a medium.

Ana pulled out a spiral-bound notebook and a pencil, and wrote Carmelita's name and the date at the top of the page. Then her hand started moving rapidly and she began scribbling so fast that she had to turn the page. As she wrote, she began to give the messages she received to Carmelita.

The spirits conveyed that Carmelita's son had recently been incarcerated. Carmelita nodded in confirmation. Since that had occurred, her daughter-in-law and grand-children had come to stay with her, and they were out of control. Carmelita felt as if she had lost control of her home.

Doña Ana continued to give more and more details of this situation, while Carmelita simply sat and listened, silently nodding her head in confirmation. Once all the messages had been delivered, Carmelita asked questions and Doña Ana flipped through her scribbled notes to find the answers.

The spirits told Carmelita how to "get things back in order." Her daughter-in-law and grandchildren were "too much for her to handle" and she was allowing her-self to be used and manipulated. There was no reason, the spirits said, that they couldn't be in their own home. Her daughter-in-law was acting like a victim and taking advantage of Carmelita, who was being "too nice." But this was affecting her health.

Doña Ana prescribed a *novena*, or nine-day prayer, to San Alejo requesting that the daughter-in-law and grandchildren go back to their own home. Once they left, Carmelita was to take a *lava pisos*, a spiritual floor wash made with herbs and essences that Doña Ana would prepare for her, and clean the floors of her home to get rid of the negativity that had been tracked in.

As for her son, *Ahi se queda* (There he'll stay) was the answer the spirits gave, meaning that they would not intervene. He would have to serve his time in jail. Apparently, he had been warned several times about his actions. In fact, Carmelita herself had delivered that warning to him on many occasions after having received it during consultations. He just didn't listen. Now he would have to pay for what he had done. Doña Ana, however, took pity on Carmelita and said: "I'll see what we can do to shorten it. *Llamame despues* (Call me later)."

Doña Ana's next client arrived only a few short minutes after Carmelita left. Rebecca was a young woman of about thirty. A previous consultation had revealed that she was the victim of a hex. Her current lover's ex had been working black magic in hopes of separating them. Unfortunately, instead of separating them, it was just causing a lot of conflict with him and with other people as well. Rebecca's visit on this day was aimed at getting rid of the hex.

Doña Ana turned to a fresh page in her notebook and, taking up her pencil, began to draw the sign of the cross as she walked all around Rebecca, praying constantly. Returning to her seat, she continued her prayers while holding the pencil on top of the notepad.

Just as before, her hand started to shake and tremble, and she started scribbling all over the paper. As this happened, she continued to pray, calling upon various saints and spiritual guides. She occasionally peppered her invocations with the words *desarrollando y levantando la causa, librandola*, unraveling and lifting the cause of negativity and freeing Rebecca from the hex.

After filling nine or ten sheets of paper, Ana's arm started moving more slowly and her writing became less frantic. Eventually, she stopped writing altogether. Then she tore the pages from the notebook and began to rub them all over Rebecca. When she had finished, she put the pages on the table, sprinkled them with various powders, and turned in all four corners to form a large package that she tied with red string. "*Entierre esto en el cementerio* (Bury this in the cemetery)," she told Rebecca. Then she handed her the package.

"*Ahora, te hare un baño pa' siete dias* (Now I'll prepare a spiritual bath for you to take for seven days)," Ana told Rebecca. Then she lifted a bowl off one of the shelves and started mixing various herbs together in it, adding some oils and several sweet-smelling perfumes. When it was ready, she filled some empty bottles with the mixture, placed them in a shopping bag, and handed the bag to Rebecca. Rebecca placed an envelope of money on the office desk as she got up to leave.

Already waiting patiently on the couch on the other side of the basement was Doña Ana's third client of the day, Santiago. He had been referred to Ana by a friend to address issues in his construction business. Apparently he wasn't getting any new contracts, even when he thought he was sure to win the bid.

As before, Ana consulted the spirits, allowing them to write using her arm. As she consulted with Santiago, I turned my own attention to her altar room, which was by far the most decorated, well-attended, and beautiful one I had ever seen. It was obvious that keeping such a sacred space demanded a great deal of time and care.

In one corner, a knee-high statue of Papa Candelo sat on the floor. He was surrounded by Papa Chango and several *madama* statues (see chapter 6). Before them sat a huge stack of apples, along with red, white, and black candles and several coffees. These were surrounded by various bouquets of flowers. A bunch of small trinkets, a small rooster, a small straw broom, a knife, and several other objects were strewn around with them.

A statue of La Dolorosa at least a foot and a half tall caught my attention next. This sat on the top shelf directly behind Ana's chair and was adorned with many rosaries and gold chains. It had a blue-and-pink candle burning before it. On its own pedestal in the corner of the room opposite me stood a large statue of St. Michael, and behind him on the shelves were other statues, including one of San Caralampio and one of San Blas.

And then I noticed something else. Although Ana's altar was glorious, there were dark spots there— areas where, although there were candles and flowers, shadows had settled and were seeping inward. I also noticed a general cloud of grayness that surrounded and followed behind Ana, as if she were covered in a gray mist. Even an *espiritista* extraordinaire must deal with both aspects of the spirit world.

Chapter 6

LOS GUIAS—SPIRITUAL GUIDES

As we have seen, *los guias*, the spiritual guides, make up a big part of the spiritual frame. They work with *espiritistas* dispensing wisdom and blessings, and give guidance, healing, and direction. These guides are also called *seres*, or beings, because they speak on behalf of God and the pure spirits. Sometimes, when speaking to someone who does not understand the culture, we call them *espiritus*, or simply spirits. In the past, it was common to hear the elders call the guides *hermanos* or *hermanas espirituales*, spiritual brothers or sisters. The term *assistentes*, or assistants, was also frequently used.

Most spiritual guides start down their path of development by acting as personal guides to an individual. Once they have helped enough people and gathered enough light, they move forward on their path and become *viejos*, meaning that they no longer serve a single individual, but can be approached by and connect with many individuals.

Spiritual guides have developed high degrees of spiritual power that make them able to help humanity. They have gone through numerous incarnations—enough so that they can choose whether to incarnate. Spiritual guides who choose to incarnate are called *guias materiales*. These are spirits of living physical elders, teachers, and mentors who have chosen to help people here on Earth directly. Those who choose not to incarnate continue to assist humanity from the spiritual realm. And as they assist, they are also assisted and continue to elevate.

The spiritual guides are divided into groups known as *commissiones*, or commissions. These groups are also called *cadenas*, or chains, and sometimes courts. Each of these chains is led by a *viejo* or *proteccion* and contains both *viejos* and *guias personales*, personal guides. The *guia principal*, which is a person's most important guide, belongs to one of these courts, but is not one of the *viejos*.

Other guides and courts of guides may come into a person's life for a particular reason or for a limited period of time to help that person with a particular issue or challenge. These guides are transient and do not form a permanent part of the person's *cuadro*. *Espiritistas*, however, generally have connections to many more guides than most, because their spiritual frames can sustain these connections. This allows them to work with many people in ways that others cannot. They can even call on guides who are not a part of their own *cuadros*.

The spiritual guides are often represented on an *espiritista's* altar by statues. Unlike statues of the saints, however, which are religious in nature, these statues are often artistic in nature and may be made to look like the various guides who are being served.

Some guides, particularly in Mesa Blanca, are represented by dolls known as *muñecas*. Most of these dolls are female, although there are a few male dolls that are used. *Muñecas* may be made by hand, like rag dolls, or may be ceramic or plastic dolls that are commercially produced. They are most often dressed in the special colors of the guide and may also have implements or accessories associated with the guide.

Muñecas act as sacred vessels for the spirit guides and their currents. Some may represent ancestors or those who have passed away. It is important to note, however, that these dolls are not used as Vodou dolls are. Rather they act as the home of the spirits and are used to connect with and attend to the spirits they are housing. Some of the most common guides that use dolls are *madamas*, Gypsies, nuns, and Indians (see below). These dolls can often be seen sitting in various places around the home on their own little chairs or benches, or on the floor, sometimes with a drink offering and a candle before them, or a large bowl or tray to collect their trinkets and gifts.

A note about terminology. The names given here for the various groups of spiritual guides are the traditional names used in Puerto Rican Espiritismo. In some cultures, however, these terms have been used to express racist sentiments, or to harm, abuse, ridicule, or discriminate against certain groups of people. For example, the term *Gypsy* is sometimes used as a pejorative rather than in its correct sense to indicate the Romani, a nomadic people that came out of the northern Indian subcontinent in the second century. This is not the case in Espiritismo, however. As used here, these terms carry no negative meaning or implications.

Following are some of the courts of spirit guides with which *espiritistas* work.

Arabes (Arabs)

The Arabic spirits hold the keys to the magic of Arabia. They know the magical and spiritual secrets of the realms of the *djinn*—spirits similar to angels but of a lower ranking who are able to appear in various forms and possess humans. They relate to the magic power of the names of Allah and of pre-Islamic magic and culture. Arabia, like all parts of the world, had ancient Pagan and magical traditions long before the arrival of Islam.

The Arabic spirits are less commonly seen these days. They can reveal the secrets of magical writing. In the past, *espiritistas* often invoked *El Gran Arabe* whenever using magical writing to break a magical spell. These spirits are often represented on altars by the bust of a man wearing a large white turban. Other items frequently found on these altars include images of camels, decorative cloths, and ceramic plates, all of which are used in the magic of the Arabic spirits.

Chamanes (Shamans)

Los chamanes are the spirits of shamans, spiritual teachers, priests, gurus, and wise men. In their hands, they hold the secrets to tribal magic, wisdom, and healing. They come from many different backgrounds and from many different cultures. They teach "how to walk in both worlds," meaning how to live in balance in both the physical and spiritual worlds. Various types of shamans exist in this court, the most widely known being the *behique*, the shaman of the native Taino people. However, this court also includes African shamans, who are sometimes called witch doctors.

Many of the shamanic spirits heal physical and spiritual ailments. They also work on soul retrievals and deal with soul loss. When we experience a sudden trauma or unexpected shock, it can dislodge a part of our soul or spirit. This can cause mental and psychological issues that have no physical component that can be identified or resolved by Western medicine. Over time, other physical ailments may develop as well. In fact, trauma can allow negative energies and spirits to take hold and these can attract other *causas* over time.

Shamans have the power to teach about astral journeying and vision questing. They can help those who have these faculties to develop them and learn to work with them. They can also bestow the ability to understand omens and signs that come through nature. Many of them work with herbs and animals, forming medicine out of both.

Don Nico, one of my own spiritual assistants, once told me: *Somos un aire; quien nos aguanta?* (We are like a fragrance; who can hold us?) By this beautiful and deeply meaningful statement, he meant that our existence is like a fragrance that must be experienced. We can try to convey this experience to others, but they must "taste" it for themselves in order to understand it. Moreover, a fragrance does not last forever. It fades; it dissolves. So it must be experienced while it lasts, or we will miss it. And this is how we learn from the *chamanes*—by experiencing their lessons ourselves, by "tasting" the balance they teach.

Madamas (Nannies)

Perhaps the most famous of all the guides are the *madamas*, the nannies. In her many forms, the *Madama* is one of the strongest figures ever to arise from the tradition. This court holds many secrets and occupies a place a major importance and impact in Puerto Rican Espiritismo.

In the old days in Puerto Rico, before slavery was abolished, children from wealthy homes were often raised by enslaved nannies. Not only was this nanny tasked with raising her master's children, but often her own as well, some of whom may well have been fathered by the master. In addition to these responsibilities, she was often charged with managing the house, overseeing all aspects of the cooking and cleaning, and taking general care of the household. *Madamas* thus hold the secrets of kitchen witchery, as well as those of herbal medicine and home cures.

In the past, *espiritistas* had special dolls made to represent this guide. These were almost always made of cloth and wore various dresses, depending on their nature. They were then prepared in a special baptism ritual and certain implements and herbs, known as a *carga,* or charge, were sewn into them. Today, you can find an assortment of *madamas* statues wearing different colors, carrying various implements, or making different gestures, each corresponding to specific natures and talents.

Doña Juana had a beautiful cloth *madama* doll when she was growing up. The doll had two dresses, and each week we changed her dress and washed the one she had previously worn by hand. She had her own little rocking chair, and regularly moved from place to place around the house. One of her favorite places to sit was by an old yellow telephone that had a twisted cord that stretched out about fifteen feet. She sat right behind the phone with a glass of coffee and water before her. She was always ready to work.

Every *madama* has a different specialty. Some are herbalists; some work with water and are specialists at cleansings; others work with fire and are excellent at bringing in protection. All *madamas* are known for their skills at healing, cleansing, fortune-telling, and bringing luck.

Madama is so beloved because she tells it straight—like a tough-talking, very blunt grandmother. Although she loves you, she will not hold back from giving you a lashing if that is what it takes to get through to you. She loves black coffee and cigars, and it is also common to see her with a tin can filled with water and certain herbs.

Many people also keep a special broom made of straw with which she performs cleansings.

In recent times, there has been some controversy around the image of the *madama*. Many feel that her image is racist, especially in the United States, where figures resembling this spirit have been used in racist ways. However, for Puerto Rican *espiritistas*, this is not the case. Instead, her image has always been given a high degree of respect and reverence.

There is also some controversy over who has the right to work with this spirit court. Some feel that the *Madama* is exclusive to the islands and that only those who have an ancestral heritage of slavery should serve her. This is also untrue. In many parts of the world, including the American South, the figure of an enslaved Black woman who managed the master's house and raised his children was common. And, just as in Puerto Rico, many children in these cultures became closer to and developed a deeper connection with their nannies than they did with their parents.

Madamos (Butlers)

Because *madamas* usually get all the attention, the spirits of the wise butlers and assistants to the powerful have been mostly forgotten. But all powerful people need a trusted advisor who has their backs through thick and thin. And this is the *madamo*. He looks out for his people and guides them toward the wisest decision for themselves.

Madamos are often represented on the altar by a statue of a man in a black suit with a perfect mustache, sitting close to the front, always ready to help and attend. Aside from being trusted advisors, they are ready to clean and clear negativity from those who work with them. They are also skilled at helping people manage life and balance the many things that must be accomplished.

Religiosos (Religious Ones)

This court includes the spirits of priests, rabbis, nuns, monks, and all those who spent their lives following and promoting a religious path. The monks and nuns teach about the path of connecting to the Divine. They assist in spiritual cleansing and purification, and reflect the Catholic approach to life.

This court encompasses the various priesthoods of all organized religions—including Christian, Jewish, Muslim, and Buddhist. They teach discipline, organization, and order, and are known to be a bit judgmental at times. Although they are often represented on the altar, these guides like to be a bit separated from other guides.

King Solomon, who was famed for his magical and spiritual capacities, is one of the *viejos* of this court. He was renowned for his wisdom, but he was also known to have power over negative spirits.

Sanaciónes (Healing Guides)

One of the most popular courts among *espiritistas* are the healing guides, who assist with all levels of spiritual, physical, and mental health. Although all the spirits within Espiritismo have the power to heal, these spirits often deal with medicine in the Western sense. They are also excellent at helping to diagnose illnesses. Some were doctors, surgeons, and other medical practitioners in life; some have been known to perform actual surgeries while mounted in a medium (see chapters 7 and 11). Others have been known to give psychic surgery, which is a spiritual removal without any physical incisions.

Doctor Jose Gregorio Hernandez is one of the *viejos* of this court. A living doctor who practiced in Venezuela in the 1900s, he is frequently found on the altar wearing a black suit and carrying a doctor's bag. He is known to be a very friendly and approachable spirit who is willing to help anyone who is ill. On the altar, he is given white candles, a glass of water, and a single white flower.

Doctor German is another well-known *viejo* of this court. Having been a surgeon in life, he can come through a medium in order to perform psychic surgery. He was quite famous as the surgeon of the poor.

Piratas y Marineros (Pirates and Sailors)

These guides assist in finding that which is hidden or, in the case of the pirates, buried. *Piratas* locate hidden treasure and help people who are downtrodden or dealing with hard times or rough seas. They are known to fight for those who have no other defenses. Remember: In the history of Puerto Rico, pirates were a very real presence.

Marineros, or sailors, are all about guidance and direction, and learning to deal with life and navigate through its many situations. They are powerful allies when it comes to gaining courage, fearlessness, and strength.

This spirit court enjoys maritime themes on its altars. They are given blue, white, and black candles, and enjoy gin, whiskey, and rum. On the altar, it is quite common to see a vessel of salt water to make them feel at home.

Indios (Indians)

The Taino and Arawak Indians who inhabited the Caribbean islands before the Europeans came to the area have had a major influence on the healing techniques of Mesa Blanca. And although many of the names of the Taino deities have been lost, the spirits of the *Indios* have remained a part of the tradition. Images of these gods and personal spiritual guides were originally carved out of stone, and the

Taino believed that these stones, called *cemis,* became vessels for the spirits. Sometimes these images were also made of wood, bone, and pottery.

The care and maintenance of the Taino gods and their *cemi* stones came under the direction of the *behique,* or shaman. But ancestral spirits and nature spirits, which also inhabited stones, were often cared for by individuals, especially warriors, who usually carried at least one of these carved stones with them. *Cemis* were commonly passed down from generation to generation, and they were also collected as prizes of war that amplified the victors' power by adding to the number of spirits working for them.

When someone receives or finds a *cemi* stone, it is a major indicator of the presence of one of the Indians in their *cuadro* (remember Titi Berta's tale). It isn't uncommon for *brujos* to find these stones and they often call out to them. *Cemi* stones are also known to whistle, to talk, and to get hot or sweat. They are commonly used in healing, and they have the power to draw out illness as well as instill healing medicine. The most prized are made of stalagmites, stalactites, and green stones.

Rather than have their *cemis* taken by European invaders, many Indians went into the woods and buried them. In fact, many of these stones have been discovered over time and are now in museums all over the island. Petroglyphs suggesting that secret rituals were performed by the Taino have been found in caves, which were very sacred to the Indians. The remnants of the Taínos and their religious traditions have thus left visible marks all over the Caribbean and in many subsequent cultures.

As spirit guides, the *Indios* are known for their aggressiveness, their courage, and their strength. They are possessive about those they guard and are always very alert, keeping a close watch over their devotees. Although the spirits in this court share these characteristics, each one has its own attributes.

Since this court is so large, it is divided into several sub-groups called legions, or columns by some. Each legion is headed by an Indian who carries its name, and spirits within each legion share certain qualities or characteristics.

- *Indios del agua* (Indians of water). Indians in this legion are adept at clearing curses and providing clarity. When they work through mediums, they often use water or perfumes in their cures. The Taino culture was very connected to water. They frequently traveled from island to island by boat and their communities were always near natural sources of water. Bathing, for both hygiene and ceremonial purposes, was one of their major activities. It is said that many of them spent more than four hours a day in bathing rituals, swimming, and in contact with water.

- *Indios del monte* (Indians of the woods). This legion teaches survival as well as herbalism. Many *Indios*, even outside of this legion, work extensively with herbs.

- *Indios de la paz* (Indians of peace). Members of this legion are old grandfathers of great wisdom, often represented by a seated Indian. This legion works to promote peace.

- *Indios de la pluma blanca* (Indians of the white feather). This legion contains all the Indian chiefs and chieftesses not found in other legions. They are often seen wearing a headdress.

- *Indios bravos* (wild Indians). These Indians are sometimes called *locos*, meaning they can be quite savage. They are the ones who resisted being subjugated by the European settlers by any means. This legion hosts some of the most popular figures, including *Indios poderosos* (powerful Indians) and *Indios de la fuerza* (Indians of power or force).

- *Indios guerrero* (Indian warriors). This legion is known to carry all types of implements of war. *Indios valientes* (brave Indians) are major figures in this legion.

- *Las Indias* (all female Indians). This legion rules over love, art, and poetry, as well as other things. *La India Luisa*, a famous female Taino chieftess who was also known as a witch is a member of this legion.

Tobacco, water, and stones are among the most common offerings for this court. Strong dark coffee, *mabi* (tea made of root bark), and rum are also given to them, and they enjoy *sahumerios*, the burning of herbs as incense. Their altars are kept on the floor and occasionally outside. They are often represented by images and statues of Native Americans. Unlike the images of saints or African deities, the Indians must have their own area on the altars.

Angeles (Angels)

The celestial angels—the "nine choirs"—comprise this court. When working with the angels, *espiritistas* ask for divine healing and clarity. This court, or chain, of spirits is massive. Angels can be called upon depending upon their specialities. Various angels of ceremonial magic can be found here, as well as the four Archangels.

In Espiritismo, everyone is known to have a guardian angel who is separate and different from their patron saint and their other spiritual guides. Your guardian angel is with you from birth till death. He or she guards your body and your mind. The guardian angel is not a member of the nine choirs, but is rather one of the angels working here on Earth.

Santos (Saints)

Unlike many other Caribbean traditions, the saints in Puerto Rican Espiritismo were served and seen in the same way as the saints of the Catholic Church. They were not used to mask African deities brought to the island by slaves. Because of this, and because of the highly effective campaign waged by the Catholic Church, much of the knowledge of African and native deities in Puerto Rico was lost.

Nonetheless, most Puerto Rican *espiritistas* have a patron saint whom they identify as their main spirit. This spirit performs an executive and protective function, acting like a guardian or overseer who guides and protects everything that goes on. This spirit does not usually work through mediums, although it can. Rather it is the *guia* who speaks on behalf of this more powerful force.

Alongside the patron saint, *espiritistas* may also work with any number of other saints, each of which has particular skills it can bring to bear on particular situations. Saints are generally friendly and amicable spirits who are easy to approach and willing to help. Each saint has its own number, day of the week, color, and offerings, and every saint has a particular feast day in the calendar year.

Virtually every Puerto Rican town or city has a patron saint as well. On that saint's feast day, huge celebrations are held in the towns, with parades, carnivals, food, games, and much more. Many *espiritistas* also celebrate the patron saint associated with the place from which they come. *Brujos* commonly hold *veladas* in honor of their patron saints on their feast days as well.

Gitanas y Gitanos (Gypsies)

This court includes both *Gitanas* (female Gypsies) and *Gitanos* (male Gypsies), but male Gypsies are less common than their female counterparts. The Gypsies that are known in Sanse are the spirits of those known to have traveled from Spain to Puerto Rico. Many of them excelled in the arts of entertainment, magic, and mystery. Some Gypsy guides are quite well known, like Esmeralda and Salome.

People often get the wrong idea about Gypsies. Also known as the Roma or Romani, they are traditionally a nomadic people who wander from place to place—but not necessarily by choice. Throughout the centuries, the Gypsy have been discriminated against by just about everyone.

Gypsy guides bring about swift and sudden change. They embrace this change as well. They are known for their prophetic abilities and divination skills, so their altar space may contain crystal balls, tarot cards, playing cards, and other divination tools. They can help develop the faculties of scrying and prophesy. Many Gypsies are also excellent readers of the Tarot. They know how to work with the cards in order to bring clarity and resolution. They can also work with the pendulum and palmistry.

People who have this court of guides in their *cuadro* often feel the need for regular change. They can become bored easily and often find themselves attracted to mystery. Without regular change, they may feel trapped by life. Like real-life Gypsies, they are often discriminated against for being different.

This can be good, or it can be bad. It all depends on whether your Gypsies have been given the proper light. On the negative side, you may be unable to create real roots or to settle down and stabilize your life. You may find yourself constantly running from one situation to the next and never growing or developing.

On the other hand, this court can help you accept and flow with life. After all, the one constant in life is change. When Gypsies have the right light, they can help their followers find the silver lining in every cloud. They can lead you to hidden solutions and opportunities when others see only problems or obstacles.

Gypsy guides are by nature very romantic and are often romanticized in modern perceptions or lore. They can help people deal with affairs of the heart, with relationships, and with passion, and can perform immensely powerful *trabajos* (workings) for those who need help in their love lives. But they are also skilled at helping people with financial opportunities and abundance—perhaps because every time they move, they must find new work. They are masters at business and can talk people into almost anything.

Gypsies love jewelry and small trinkets. Think of the brightly colored cloths and the overwhelming abundance found inside a Gypsy caravan. These guides are served with most colors—white, red, and black, but also green, gold, and purple. They love liquor and drinks, and are especially fond of whiskey and champagne. They are also frequently smokers.

Orientales (Orientals)

This court is composed of the Asian spiritual masters, Buddhas, and guides. Among them there are also great warriors who are very precise in slicing through ignorance in order to open space for wisdom. The leader of this court is the *Buddha Otai* (Hotei)—a fat, happy Buddha who is surrounded by gold and jewels. He bestows good luck and fortune, financial and material success, and abundance. He is said to have a huge influence on Fortuna, the spirit of fortune also known as Lady Luck. Because of this, many people approach the guides of this court when they are looking for luck in the lottery and or in games of chance

It is common to find a large Buddha, sometimes surrounded by other smaller Buddhas, set up on an *espiritista's* altar. These can also be found in other areas of the homes of *espiritistas* and their followers to bring money and luck into the dwelling.

When Puerto Rico was owned by Spain, the Spanish encouraged immigration of non-Hispanic people to the island. This was intended to attract more Europeans, particularly Catholics, but ended up attracting Chinese and other Asian immigrants. Chinese laborers and those fleeing China were already present on many of the Caribbean islands. In 1882, when the United States enacted a law that prohibited the immigration of Chinese laborers, many Chinese came instead to Puerto Rico and Cuba. Later, when the United States acquired Puerto Rico and conducted a census, they decided to document the Chinese as a separate group. Then in the 1950s, more waves of Chinese fled to Puerto Rico as a result of the Cuban revolution.

This court of spiritual guides does not usually work through mediums. In fact, I have seen very few of them come through in this way. For the most part, these guides prefer to communicate spiritually with mediums to provide wisdom and guidance. Most of them have a very subtle, serene energy.

One of my encounters with an oriental guide was with an elderly man who had passed his guide through—Maestro Lu Chen. When he came through the medium, it was as subtle as a gentle spring breeze, and many did not notice it right away. His message was simple: Do not forget.

Lu Chen explained the sin of forgetfulness, saying that most of our sins are committed by simply forgetting what is important. At these words, a woman seated in the back of the room burst into tears, while another burst out laughing—each reacting differently to the sudden revelations and epiphanies they had received from the words of this wise spiritual master.

This court is attended to on the altar with citrus fruits, especially oranges. They also love incense of all types, and are happy when given lottery tickets, dice, gold coins, and other bright shiny objects. Mediums burn orange, pink, or red candles on the altar in their honor.

Encantos (Enchantments)

Los encantos, or enchantments, are spirits who never actually had living incarnations. Instead, they are beings from the spiritual world who are connected to the elements.

Kongos (Congolese)

It is estimated that over 80 percent of the enslaved Africans brought to Puerto Rico came from the Congo, so it makes perfect sense that these spirits have their own court. Like the Taino who inhabited the island before them, these new arrivals also believed in their own gods and spirits, and had a rich spiritual tradition and practice back in Africa.

Like the Taino, the Kongo portrayed their deities as large over-arching forces, but also acknowledged that individuals had personal spiritual allies who assisted them. This is similar to the way in which espiritistas work with patron saints and personal guides. In fact, many of the guides best known today come from this court.

The guides of this court are known to be incredibly fierce and protective. They can break and reverse negative energy, witchcraft, and hexes. They are extremely loyal to those with whom they work, and quick to punish. They are often strict and so are often called on for justice.

This court is known for its warriors. They love the colors black and red, although they are at times also given brown, orange, and green. Many spirits of this court are avid herbalists who know how to work with herbs for both magic and healing. Most enjoy cigars and rum, as well as bitter black coffee.

Esclavos (Slaves)

Los esclavos are the spirits of elevated slaves who come to teach about various topics. Some teach of courage and leadership, and of what it takes to make change. Others share the wisdom of humility and peace, and of how to change our plights. These spirits have chosen to return to bring healing and wisdom, and to restore balance.

Slaves came to Puerto Rico from all over Africa, and this court contains spirits from many tribes—but not the Kongo, who have their own court because they were so numerous. The colors of this court are black and white. They enjoy black coffee and water, as well as cigars; they are often given bread.

Juanes y Marias (Johns and Marys)

The *Juanes y Marias* are a huge court of spirits who assist *brujos* in all sorts of *trabajos*. *Juan* is the Spanish equivalent of the name John; *Maria* is the equivalent of Mary. During the time when Spanish Catholics were forcing the conversion of both natives and slaves, one of their main practices was to give them new names in order to further split them away from their identities. Since they cared extraordinarily little for them as individuals, they often baptized them in large groups, giving them all the new names Juan and Maria.

This shared name was usually followed by a descriptive term to distinguish one slave from another. Thus a slave who showed an aptitude for money and finances might be called "John the money man"; another who was known for being romantic might be called "John the lover"; another who was a particularly hard worker might be called "John the worker." The same was true for women, who acquired names like "Mary the cook" or Mary the singer."

This court is vast, containing spirits who are invoked by *brujos* in *trabajos* in which they specialize. *Espiritistas* often use cigars when working with them.

Negras y Africanas (Blacks and Africans)

This court is made up of all those who worked with, served, or were initiated into the various African-based religions that made their way to the Caribbean. Many of these spirits are priests and priestesses of Santeria, Palo Mayombe, the 21 Divisions, and Haitian Vodou. They are sometimes called *la commission Santera* or the Santeria commission.

Commonly, these spirits can be found in the *cuadros* of those whose ancestors practiced one of these other traditions or were initiated into them. It is also common for these spirits to aspire to become initiated in one of these religions themselves.

This court works with the *Siete Potencias*, or the Seven African Powers, which are extremely popular among *espiritistas*. These seven powers are invoked for protection, court cases, and general blessings. They also correspond to the seven major *orishas* (elevated spirits) of the Cuban Santeria tradition: Obatala, Chango, Yemaya, Oshun,

Oya, Eleggua, and Ogun. In fact, of the all the *orishas* of Cuban Santeria, it was these seven who would be incorporated by Mesa Blanca *espiritistas*. They would become the major focus of those practicing Santerismo, a religion formed from the blending of Santeria and Espiritismo.

IS THERE A RABBI IN THE HOUSE?

At one time, I was called in by a Muslim family who were experiencing many issues in their home. Whenever friends and family visited, things broke for no reason and all types of calamities and conflicts occurred. After ruling out everything physical, they brought in an imam (a Muslim priest) to bless the house, as well as another spiritualist who tried to clear the home. Nothing seemed to work. Or more accurately, at first things seemed to work, but after a short while, the problems came back with a fury and were even worse. That was when they knew something else was at play, but they just couldn't get to the bottom of it.

The family was referred to me by a friend, and I came to their home to see what I could do. After doing a thorough search of the home, I found that they had the spirit of a rabbi living there. I advised them to commission a rabbi to come to their home and give a traditional prayer ritual. Only then could I return and get them settled.

A few weeks later, the Muslim couple came across the previous owners of the home, who confirmed that they had also experienced strange occurrences in the house while they lived there. When asked if they knew if any

ESPIRITISMO

Jewish people had ever lived in the house, they confirmed that they had purchased the home from a Jewish man who was the son of a rabbi. Apparently, he had inherited the house when his father, the rabbi, died.

Never underestimate the power of the spirits.

Chapter 7

COMMUNICATING WITH THE SPIRIT WORLD

A medium is someone who has the capacity to communicate and work with the spiritual world. Mediums can consciously act as channels for the spirits and their communications, but for them to do so, that capacity has to be activated. Although we all have this latent power, it remains inactive in most of us. Thus most people are not mediums. Moreover, although all mediums are *espiritistas,* not all *espiritistas* are mediums, simply because they have not developed their capacity to communicate consciously and work with the spiritual planes. Allen Kardec, the founder of Scientific Spiritism, was not a medium at all, although he was an *espiritista.*

There are many ways to activate the power of mediumship. In fact, many mediums are born with this power already activated to some degree or another. This usually means that they have experiences with the spirit world at an early age. Unfortunately, throughout the course of their lives, these abilities can become deactivated. Others may have their mediumistic abilities activated as the result of some life experience—perhaps an experience with the spiritual world, or perhaps a trauma or some other negative experience. Some mediums even find that their faculties open after having been attacked spiritually by another medium, an experience that can be very detrimental and can drive people crazy if they have not developed the proper mechanisms for dealing with these powers.

Some mediums inherit an active faculty of mediumship from a loved one or a relative. Others succeed at opening up latent faculties through purposeful study and practice. And those with latent mediumistic abilities can even become activated just by being around other mediums whose abilities are highly developed.

TYPES OF MEDIUMSHIP

Most mediums practice their art in order to pursue personal awakening and enlightenment. This is, after all, the ultimate goal of each individual soul. Through their mediumship, mediums find their purpose in life and fulfill it, and then go on to live a life filled with blessings.

A great number of mediums are mediums *de causa*, or causal mediums, who can interact with a negative spirit in order to remove it (see below). These mediums are faced with a huge task, because they have a natural tendency to attract causal spirits who can and often do infect the mediums with their own illnesses, especially when the mediums are underdeveloped or untrained (see chapter 10).

Some mediums are *muerteros* or *muerteras*, mediums who have a special capacity for communicating with the dead or even acting as conduits for them (see below). These mediums can help heal ancestral and family trauma, and can help bring closure and healing to loved ones. Many of them also have the capacity to connect with the dead and with the guides. These mediums are skilled at helping people deal with hauntings and other problems with the dead. It is quite common for them to fear the dead or their own gifts until they become more developed.

Other mediums are meant to work for healing the spirits, rather than working for living people. They help spirits who are suffering, who tend to seek them out. These mediums focus on *levantando los muertos,* or lifting the dead. This can often be very heavy and tiresome work, as many of these spirits can be very insistent and bothersome. Most of these mediums are dedicated to suffering souls and their plight, and this is where they focus their efforts and work.

DESARROLLO (UNRAVELING)

A medium's abilities are always a work in progress. They must be worked with, developed, and polished in order to shine. This process of spiritual development is known as *desarrollo,* or unraveling. Development is also sometimes called *evolución,* meaning evolution or progress. Without proper development, a medium's faculties remain in a raw form, and this can cause many problems for newly activated mediums. Many novice mediums find themselves experiencing depression, fatigue, anxiety, and even physical health conditions. Their relationships and lives can be negatively affected.

Underdeveloped mediums who use their faculties before they are ready often find themselves plagued with a whole host of issues that they take on from others. The mediumistic faculty acts as a natural magnet for spirits—both pure and impure—and negative energies will take advantage of this when they can. Some developing mediums may even feel as if they are losing their minds. When a faculty is activated suddenly through some tragic event, it can leave them totally open to constant bombardment by spirits and regular harassment. If this is allowed to continue, it can cause many other problems, some of which can have physical consequences.

Underdeveloped faculties can also bring on financial blockages, as the spirits may close off avenues to success. In fact, many mediums experience their new abilities almost as a curse because of all the problems their underdeveloped faculties can cause. Although mediumistic abilities can at times bring in certain blessings, it is not uncommon for them to bring in harm.

For the community at large, working with underdeveloped mediums often creates as many problems as it resolves. Clients can find themselves misguided, misdirected, and in a world of trouble. Because they may not be able to resolve the causal issue properly, novice mediums may unwittingly fix with one hand and destroy with the other, without even knowing they are doing so.

Novice mediums begin their unravelment through study, apprenticeship, and practice. Once they become aware of their abilities, they begin to look for a *guia material*, or material guide—a highly developed medium known as a *padrino* (godfather) or *madrina* (godmother) who acts as teacher, mentor, and spiritual master. These mentors have highly developed mediumistic powers that allow them to lead, teach, and unravel other mediums. They are also known as *mayores* or *viejos*—elders or old ones.

Once aspiring mediums have found a *padrino*, they undergo training and education on how to handle and develop their faculties. They are also given practices and work to do in order to further develop their skills. They attend specific rituals and are shown how to connect with their *cuadros,* as well as how to discern the nature of various types of spirits. Once mediums have started the process of *desarrollo*, they become less prone to harm. Rather than experiencing their faculties as a curse, they start to receive blessings, understanding, and wisdom through them and begin to find and live their purpose.

Many mediums, after some development, have the capacity to help themselves and live a blessed life. For most, this is the purpose of their mediumship. Once they begin to unravel their faculties, they are able to give back to others by assisting their *padrinos* and participating in group rituals. This encourages their unravelment and gives them a chance to put their skills into practice. It also gives them a chance to serve others in a safe, protected, and sacred space. Under the watchful eye of the elders, they are guided and supported in their growth and development.

Any act or job can become a spiritual one. This is one of the most important lessons for new mediums to learn. When mediums are fulfilling the purpose given to them, rather than one they try to force or to choose themselves, they find success both spiritually and in life. Being a medium is not the only spiritual path. Every life path has a purpose and *is* a purpose. It is important to understand this. Many mediums, after discovering or developing their abilities, end up suffering problems and issues simply because they try to do spiritual work for others when they are called to do something else.

While I was growing up, I attended hundreds of *veladas* where people communicated with the spirits all the time. I witnessed and received messages regularly. But I was always just an observer at these rituals, not a medium. When it came time for me to participate as a student medium, I was terrified.

Much to my pleasure and happiness, I was given a seat all the way at the back of the room and told to watch the whole session. As each person came up, I was to take notes on what came to me about the person. I was also told to focus my mind and concentrate intently while saying the prayers.

So that's what I did. And I discovered that almost everyone in the back row was a "medium in development," but I had never noticed it until that day. This is when the *velada* took on a new meaning for me, and I began paying more attention to every detail. I began to notice things that I hadn't before, probably because my eyes were starting to become more and more open to the spiritual world.

FACULTADES (FACULTIES)

Several abilities must become active in order for mediums to communicate with the spirits and the spiritual realms. These spiritual abilities or talents are called *facultades* (faculties) and sometimes *luces,* or lights. In essence, it is by activating these faculties that a medium becomes a medium.

Faculties often start in a raw form and must be trained and developed, just like muscles. When novice mediums are told to *desarrollar sus luces,* they are being told to begin the process of unraveling their faculties. A faculty that has been well developed is called a *luz desarrollada.* As mediums work to unravel, new and latent faculties begin to awaken.

The initial capacities and abilities of mediumship are spiritual gifts, but the strength and power of these gifts must be earned. This is the result of many lifetimes of work and development. Only once these faculties are developed can mediums begin to receive *videncias,* or messages from the spirits. As mediums' faculties develop, the messages they receive gain in clarity and accuracy, and their ability to be more descriptive and vivid in passing on these messages grows.

Some faculties enable communication with the spirits, while others assist in dealing with the spiritual world. Some of these faculties may be more prominent than others, and mediums are often classified by one of their more prominent communicative faculties.

Videntes, or clairvoyants, are those who have visions of the spirits or see messages as images. These may sometimes be single images and sometimes multiple images that play out like short movie clips. They may be either symbolic or literal. Mediums must develop their capacity to interpret and decipher these visual messages correctly.

Clairaudient mediums, on the other hand, hear the voices of the spirits. The messages they receive are auditory in nature. By contrast, clairsentient mediums *feel* the currents and the spirits. Although all mediums have this ability to some degree, for clairsentient mediums, this is the primary faculty they rely upon. Clairsentient mediums feel—emotionally, mentally, or physically—the energy, current, or spirit. Following the trail of bread crumbs, so to speak, from one feeling to another, they unravel their messages for those for whom they are meant.

Empaths are another type of medium found in this category. Most people have some degree of empathy; but empaths have a higher degree of sensitivity to others' energy, pain, or emotions. In fact, they may often find themselves being "infected" with it. Unless they develop this faculty, it can cause issues. Once developed, however, they can use it without it causing other problems for themselves or for others.

I also call this faculty *sabiendo,* or knowing. Mediums don't necessarily know how they know what they know. They can't necessarily pinpoint how they understand the messages they receive; they simply *know.* Sometimes you just know what you know. You have no need for physical evidence; you just *know*. Deep down in your core. Just like anything else, however, this sense of knowing can be false. So just as with other mediumistic faculties, this one must be cleared and developed as well.

The faculty of *la clave* (literally, the key) was one of the most popular ways to communicate with the spirits, especially in the beginning of Espiritismo. In the West, this is known as automatic writing. This was Doña Ana's main faculty. When I was growing up, I remember many mediums used *la clave* to receive and pass on messages.

In *la clave*, the spirits take control of the arm and hand of the medium and write their messages. Sometimes these messages are written in words; sometimes they appear as scribble scrabble that only the medium can read and interpret. Sometimes the writing comes in so fast that the medium barely has a chance to turn the page. *La clave* was also used to heal, as well as to make magic.

Along with these primary faculties, the spirits also communicate through the vehicle of smells and scents, causing the medium to sense fragrances that aren't actually present. Mediums may also feel pains or touches on their bodies, which can be caused by spirits of either the living or the dead.

Most mediums have several faculties, each operating at a different level of strength or light. And the faculties that mediums have determine what they can do. By combining the information received from all their faculties, mediums are able to convey messages from the spirits. But the ability to decipher, interpret, and understand these messages is also an important faculty. In fact, all mediums must work to develop this skill, because receiving messages is useless if they don't understand them. This is all part of the work that goes into developing the *cuadro*.

PASAR LOS SERES
(PASSING THE SPIRITS)

Although all types of mediumship require trance, those called trance mediums are actually *montado* (mounted) by the spirits or *pasan* (pass) the spirits through their bodies. When a medium mounts or passes the spirit, the spirit takes over the body of the medium, which then serves as a vessel for it. In this way, the spirits can communicate with people directly. Trance mediums allow the spirits to use their bodies as vehicles for communication and this is one of the most popular forms of mediumship in Espiritismo.

In Mesa Blanca, there are several types of trance mediums. As with most faculties, many mediums can perform more than one type of trance mediumship. In fact, most trance mediums can undergo the various types depending on the will of the spirits and the scenario at hand. Here are the three most common types:

- *Trance asombrao* (overshadowed). In this type of trance, the medium is *consiente,* or conscious, and aware of everything that is going on. The spirit, in a sense, sits on top of the medium like a shadow and controls the medium's actions and speech. But the medium can push back through at any time.

- *Trance media unidad* (halfway unity). This type of trance occurs when mediums are semi-conscious during the time the spirits are using their bodies. Mediums may go in and out of consciousness throughout the event. Since they go in and out of consciousness, they remember some portions of what has happened and may not know other portions. This is the most common type of trance. The good spirits commonly use it during consultations because it allows them to take partial control over the medium's body and vocal cords, so they can speak their *videncias,* or messages, directly. They can also use this type of trance to "work" or heal the person by taking control of the medium's limbs and other extremities.

- *Trance inconsiente* (unconscious). This type of trance occurs when mediums are totally unaware of everything once the spirit has taken control over their bodies. The spirit of the medium actually enters a dream-like state and is pushed into the astral realms. While in the astral realms, the medium may learn things about the spirits and the spiritual world. Because the communicating spirit takes full control over the medium's body, the medium retains no memory of the events. In these cases, mediums often rely on an assistant when working for others so they can know which spirits are working through them, eventually learning to recognize the various currents present to assist the spirit, the medium, and the client.

Trances asombraos and *trances media unidades* are also used to teach mediums. By allowing them to witness the work or information that comes through their mentors, novice mediums learn the various ways in which the spirit works with them. They can also learn directly about the currents and about healing.

When trance mediumship occurs, either the medium or the spirit often marks it in some way—perhaps by ringing a bell whenever the spirit is coming through to speak. The bell will also ring again once control has been returned to the medium so that the client knows when the spirit is speaking and when the medium is speaking. Another way this is handled is by a key phrase being spoken whenever the spirit begins to speak.

Trance mediumship is quite common and popular in Espiritismo. Many prefer it, believing it to be "clearer." This is not necessarily the case, although it can very often be so. Among the elders, however, it is well known that well-developed mediums have no need for full-on trances most of the time. Trance mediumship is very tiring and can be stressful on mediums' bodies and minds. To some degree, it can be healing; however, in many ways, it is extremely taxing. Just as other mediums who find their abilities elsewhere should work on developing their trance mediumship, so natural trance mediums should work on developing their other faculties.

SPIRITUAL CENTERS

Spiritual centers, known as *centros*, are the home base of all group work. These are also called *templos*, or temples. Since the late 1800s, separate temples and centers have been built for the practice of Espiritismo all over the island of Puerto Rico and elsewhere. During the early 1900s, there was a huge growth in the number of Kardecist *centros* as well as those of Mesa Blanca. From the late 1940s through today, these centers also popped up in the back of *botanicas* (spiritual supply stores) and *bodegas* (Hispanic convenience stores).

Before the late 1800s, most Espiritismo rituals or ceremonies were held in the homes of their leaders—not in a dedicated space, but in an emptied-out living room, dining room, or garage. And this practice continues today. What makes a space a *centro* is not so much where the space is as what happens there. Wherever group rituals happen or people congregate for spiritual purposes, the place is acting as a *centro*.

Centros are also the home base for mediums working on their development. There, mediums can work on developing their faculties under proper guidance and the watchful eye of the elders. Service at the *centro* is one of the most common ways for mediums to *hacer caridad*, or give back to the community, sharing the blessings they have received from the spirits.

For the congregation, *centros* offer the opportunity to receive messages, attain clarity, and receive healing from the spirits and mediums. There, the congregation gets the blessing of perhaps receiving messages from more than one medium or getting more than one perspective on a situation. It is also a place where *espiritistas* can find help.

Since most rituals were traditionally held in temporary spaces, they usually consisted of a simple setup of tables and chairs, and the space was properly cleansed and prepared prior to the ritual. In the case of dedicated *centros*, the room is usually plain, with images of some spirits, guides, or saints posted on the walls. They also contain an altar, or *mesa espiritual*, which may be the property of the *centro* or of the owner or leader of the *centro*. This table may have statues and images of saints and guides on it, as well as spiritual tools used by mediums, offerings, various cloths, and other ritual objects (see below). Some centers even boast small libraries with information on Espiritismo.

LA MESA ESPIRITUAL

The central focus of group rituals is a table known as the *mesa espiritual* that serves as both a ceremonial altar and as a place for the spirits to come and communicate. This table is usually, but not always, covered with a white cloth, a practice from which the Mesa Blanca tradition takes its name. In some *centros*, the table is simply white or painted white rather than having a cloth on it. For rituals conducted at home, this can also be just a dining room table covered with a white cloth.

The table usually features a large clear bowl or glass of water. This may be a fishbowl or vase as well; however, the glass must be completely clear with no markings. On larger tables, there may be more than one. This central glass of water is known as the *fuente*, or fountain (see chapter 12). The *fuente,* which serves a variety of functions, is one of the most important tools in Puerto Rican Espiritismo. All altars in Espiritismo have a *fuente,* which acts as a conduit through which the spirits communicate. Just as water conducts electricity, the *fuente* conducts the *corrientes* of the spirits. It also acts as a spiritual portal through which spirits can enter and through which mediums can direct their currents into the spiritual realms.

Mediums can use the *fuente* to scry, treating it like a crystal ball through which they receive messages from the spirits. And they can also send messages through it. The *fuente* can also be used to clear negative energies, to remove *causas,* and to heal. Since it acts as a conduit for spiritual and psychic currents, it is usually emptied after rituals, because the water collects the energies and imprints of that which has passed through it.

At least one white candle will also be present on the table to give the spirits light and to light their way. The candle is white to symbolize purity and the intent to communicate with the good spirits. Since spirits are attracted to light, the candle helps to get their attention. There can be more than one candle on the table.

Although this is all that is necessary to set up a *mesa espiritual,* the table usually also has a few other tools on it, particularly prayer books. Since the very beginning of the tradition, *brujos* and *curanderos* have used both traditional and Catholic prayers when working with and calling upon the spirits, and these have been collected in various prayer books that are used in their rituals.

Bottles of alcohol-based perfumes and colognes known as *alcoholados* and *kolonias* may also be on the table. The most common of these is Florida Water, a commercially produced cologne that has a unique citrusy semi-floral scent that you never forget. Since the early 1800s, it has been used as a household cleansing and scenting agent, as an aftershave, in the laundry, to refresh bed linens, and more.

Florida Water was one of the first perfumes available to natives and slaves, so they began offering it to the spirits. They noticed that it attracted them and that they liked it, and it also had a cleansing action, which meant that it attracted good spirits and tended to clear away negativity. Thus Florida Water became a part of native practices all over the Caribbean, the southern United States, and South America.

Flowers may be placed on the table as well, as they are agreeable to and attract good spirits. Flowers are offerings that the spirits can use to amplify their currents and to help them stabilize their forces in this realm by giving them something a bit more material with which to work.

In front of the table there is often a vessel of cleansing waters—water mixed with colognes, herbs, and flower petals. Not all tables have this, however. Likewise, in some *sessiones*, holy water or other spiritual waters are sprinkled on the participants before and/or after the ritual. And sometimes a vessel of cleansing water is placed at the door for people to use before they sit down.

Although this is the most common setup, the *mesa espiritual* can have various other arrangements, depending on the purpose of the ritual being done.

DÉJA VU

It was unbelievable. A beautiful experience of *déja vu* told me that I was in the right place. The center was almost exactly what I had grown up with—an old-style *centro*.

It was a small space that consisted of two rooms and a bathroom in the basement of a building. The *espiritistas* running it rented the space and, every Sunday, they held a public *Misa*. The entire place was painted white. On a wall was a sign that read:

Spiritual Reunion Every Sunday
Morning Service 9 AM
Spiritual Passes with Brothers & Sisters 11 AM
Silence Inside. No Cell Phones.

The room was bare except for the *mesa espiritual* set up at the front and the rows of chairs placed before it. The table was covered with a white cloth and held a single white candle, a bottle of Florida Water, and a clear glass of water. Six mediums sat behind the table, each wearing a white lab coat over their clothing. On the wall behind them hung a plastic white dove, representing the Holy Spirit.

The room was packed with congregants as a short woman with gray hair styled in a pixie cut stood up in front of the table holding a well-worn little book. She began reading the opening prayers as the congregation bowed their heads and mentally prayed with her. When she finished, she called for the *union de pensamientos*, the union of thoughts. After a few moments of silence, she slowly returned to her seat.

The mediums, with eyes closed, concentrated on the task at hand. The woman who had led the prayers sprinkled some Florida Water in each one of their hands. Some murmured prayers under their breath; others briskly rubbed their limbs; one sat as still as a stone statue. The one farthest to the right eventually started to shake lightly and spoke: "Good evening, little ones," she said in a husky male voice. Then the medium sitting next to her did the same and this continued, one by one, all the way down the row, with each spirit cleansing the medium and greeting the crowd.

Once the reunion was open, the congregation and the mediums divided into two groups. Half of the congregation and half of the mediums went to a back room that contained only a large white table with a *fuente*. The mediums sat behind the table, while the people took seats in the rows of chairs before it.

I remained in the front room, where three of the mediums had been left to carry out the work. All of them appeared to be over sixty years old. On the left sat the medium who had led the opening prayers. In the center sat a medium with a caramel complexion and long dark hair that reached to her elbow. She was wearing a white dress and gold bangle bracelets that covered most of her forearm. Each time she spoke and moved her arms, they jingled like chimes. To her left sat a short elderly male medium who wore a light-blue Guevara shirt under his lab coat and chocolate-colored dress pants with dress shoes.

The male medium began by delivering a message to a middle-aged woman in the center of the room. She was being bothered by spirits, he said, which the woman confirmed. He went on to tell her that she was unable to sleep, as well as a few other things that she had been experiencing, and recommended that she stay for magnetic healing passes at the end of the service.

The medium in the center then delivered a message to another younger lady sitting in the front. She told her that she had just suffered a loss through the suicide of a loved one. Tears started rolling down the woman's face as she nodded excitedly. She went up to the front and the medium continued to deliver the message to her in hushed tones.

One by one, various individuals were given messages. Once their initial message was delivered, they went up to the front and stood before the small white table, where the medium continued to deliver the messages that were coming through. If any of the other mediums had something to add, they did so once the first medium had finished.

Eventually, it was my turn. The medium with the bangles started shaking her arms and shivering. "You have a big light and a big *cuadro,*" she said as she rubbed her arms vigorously. "But you have a spirit of the sea. She is upset with you because you used to take care of her once a year and you didn't do it this year."

She was absolutely right.

"What you're dealing with now is happening because you haven't taken care of your obligation to her. Go take care of it."

In fact, I had been thinking about doing just that. Every year since I was eight or nine, I had gone to the sea and done a special ritual that I had been taught as a child. But this year, I had been so busy that I had completely forgotten about it. By the time I remembered, it was already fall and the weather had turned cold. Since part of the ritual requires getting wet, I was avoiding it.

Once all the messages had been delivered, a box of white envelopes was passed around the congregation to be used for donations. The collection basket followed soon after. Once the collection was complete, it was time for the closing prayers.

The elderly woman who had led the opening prayers delivered them. When the prayers were finished, we were all asked to remain seated and quiet as she went to check on the mediums in the back room. A few minutes later, she returned with the other mediums and rest of the congregation following behind her. Once everyone was back in the front room, she announced that everyone was free to leave, but those who wanted to receive spiritual passes were to stay behind. A tall elderly male medium with white hair and glasses ushered the congregation out as the rest of the mediums went to the back room.

About two months later, I asked my goddaughter about returning to the center. She informed me that, unfortunately, it had closed. Apparently the rent had been increased and they couldn't afford to continue using the space—a sad story that is all too common these days.

Chapter 8

REUNIONES Y VELADAS

The *reunion espiritual* is the primary ritual of Espiritismo. These ceremonies are also called *sessiones,* or sessions. The ritual opens the portal between the spiritual and material worlds. As such, it becomes a forum for the spirits and a workshop for their sacred work. These ceremonies are also known as *Misas espirituales,* or spiritual Masses.

In the past, it was immensely popular to have everyone sit in a circle around the central altar, which was often a dining room table, much as for a séance. This works well for smaller groups and is also commonly used in *sessiones de desarrollo,* sessions for the development of mediums. Some *espiritistas* prefer to set the altar table up against a wall with the two leading mediums sitting on either side of it and other mediums flanking them, arranged according to their degree of unravelment. In this case, the congregation is seated in a semicircle around the table and the mediums.

Some practitioners seat the mediums behind the altar table, as if they were sitting at a desk, with the *presidente,* the medium leading the reunion, in the center and the other mediums seated to the left and right, again arranged according to their spiritual development. More spiritually developed mediums sit closer to the center, while less developed mediums sit toward the ends of the table.

Regardless of the setup, the congregation sits in rows opposite the mediums, as in a church. Sometimes the room has pews or benches; sometimes it has chairs set up in rows. In the past, it was customary for men to sit on one side and women to sit on the other. Children and novice mediums always sat in the back.

The ritual starts with a series of Catholic and Spiritist prayers that set the sacred space and the intention of the ritual. They create a unity of intention in order to accomplish the sacred work. They also set the spiritual boundaries that are needed for the mediums to accomplish their task.

After these prayers, the mediums begin to cleanse themselves with passes of the hands and spiritual waters (see chapter 12). The congregation may also be invited to cleanse themselves. Then the congregation is often asked to go into a *union de pensamientos,* or union of thoughts, so that everyone can participate in silent internal prayer.

Once the stage has been set, the work can begin. This usually starts with the leading medium receiving a message from the spirits for one of the individuals present. He or she then calls that person up to the table to deliver the message and asks them to place their hands on the central bowl of water as they receive it. Any other mediums who have something to add may chime in, but only after asking for permission by knocking on the table.

Once the initial message has been given, the service begins in earnest, with mediums calling people up and delivering their messages. This continues until all the messages have been delivered. When the mediums are done receiving and delivering the spirits' messages, the lead medium calls for the closing prayers, which shut down the ritual and close the sacred space. A reunion generally lasts from two to four hours.

Several other things can happen during a reunion as well. The *presidente* or one of the mediums may do a reading and meditation on a sacred text. Testimonials to the power of God and the spirits may be spoken, with members of the congregation coming up to share their stories. Or the lead medium may give a sermon on a spiritual truth.

There are many different types of reunions. They may also have a specific purpose or be held for a particular person or group of persons. Some reunions are investigative in nature, with the purpose of digging deeply into someone's spiritual frame and life. There are also *sessiones de sanación*, or healing sessions.

Participating in reunions was a regular part of my upbringing. There were several *presidentes de mesa*, presidents of the table, in my family who commonly held these functions. And we were frequent guests at the reunions of my family's associate *espiritistas*. These reunions were commonly held on Friday or Saturday evenings.

VELADAS (VIGILS)

A *velada* is a candle vigil. The ritual is set up much like reunion or a session, but, in addition to the table where the mediums sit, there is usually another altar set up with candles. These candles may be placed on another table or on the floor. The vigil may be dedicated to a specific spirit or to all spirits in general. During a *velada*, the *mesa espiritual* is usually filled with several plates of candles, as it is an offering of light.

Veladas are usually held at night or after sunset, although this is not an absolute requirement. They are usually concluded before midnight. If a *velada* happens to continue past midnight, however, there will usually be an intermission called from midnight to 1:00 AM, because that is the hour when it is believed that all the realms open, including the negative realms. Negative spirits can thus be attracted toward the spiritual activities and attach themselves to participants. During this hour, everyone is encouraged to have a light snack and socialize. At 1:00 AM, the ritual recommences and continues until all the work is done. Only then is it closed.

Veladas can have several purposes. They can be performed as thanks to a particular spirit or as payment for some blessing obtained. They can also be offered to a spirit in order to ask for a blessing or favor. Or they can be done in order to gain clarity or uncover what is hidden.

Unlike *reuniones*, which are mainly communicative forums, *veladas* generate *fuerza*, or power. Therefore, they can be performed in order to do *trabajos pesados*, or heavier work. They can also be done to *trabajar las causas*, or work the causal spirits. This is one of the primary forms of healing in Mesa Blanca.

During *veladas*, various types of cleansings can occur, as the power is there to do them. Spiritual cleansings that occur during *veladas* are often done in the form of *barridas*, during which mediums take a handful of herbs or other items and sweep them over a person's aura. The herbs and other items have currents that act as magnets, drawing out the negativity. Mediums can also use *barridas* to give blessings, placing light into the aura rather than drawing negativity out.

I remember one occasion on which Doña Nereida performed her annual *velada* and people came from all over to participate. On this particular night, the image of Chango had been set up on a table covered with a bright red sheet. A single candle flickered before him with a crucifix, a glass of water, and a handful of cigars fanned out in a semi-circle. At the foot of the altar were rum, wine, and coffee, and an array of red flowers of various types that had been brought as offerings by those attending the ceremony.

Rows of chairs were arranged to face the altar. In a single chair at the front sat Nereida, flanked by two of her assistants. Just before 7:00 PM, everyone lined up to take a seat in the ceremonial space. Before entering, they passed between two assistants, one of whom cleansed them with incense while the other offered a bowl of spiritual holy water so that they could clear themselves. It was a powerful evening that I will never forget.

IT PAYS TO LISTEN

I was invited to a *reunion espiritual* conducted by a well-known *espiritista* in a converted one-car garage where he held *Misas* every other week.

In order to enter, I had to hop over an incense burner that was releasing copious amounts of frankincense smoke. Once inside, a medium directed me to a bucket of water into which perfume and flower petals had been mixed so I could wash my hands.

All the walls of the center were covered with images of saints, pictures of passed loved ones, Buddhas, Hindu deities, and a variety of religious icons. There was even a picture of President Clinton next to an image of the Divine Child. Sprinkled throughout were pictures of the medium's deceased relatives, many of whom had been *espiritistas* and mediums themselves. I recognized quite a few of them from my youth.

On the wall opposite the main door stood a *mesa espiritual* that stretched from one end of the garage to the other. It must have been at least twelve feet long. On it was a massive array of saints, spiritual waters and colognes, various implements, herbs, rosaries, liquors, and other ritual objects. Amid these items, here and there, were glass-encased candles that burned brightly, shedding rays of light around the space.

On the other side of table were nine mediums. They sat with closed eyes, in prayer, preparing themselves for the upcoming work. Before them on the table were three large fishbowls filled with water and two candles. Once everyone had made their way in and settled down, the president of the table lit the two candles and began to recite the opening prayers.

After the opening prayers, the lead medium went up to a small podium that was set up on the end of the table. He opened his Bible and read the story of how Abraham was asked by God to sacrifice his son. When he finished, he began to speak about faith—what it is, and what it means to have pure faith. Then he began to give his testimony to the power of the spirits. He started by telling about how he had just avoided being robbed.

"Something has happened to me here since the last reunion," he began. "You know how it is here. You don't need to lock anything up. No one is going to take any-thing. Besides, I don't have much to take anyway." He laughed.

"But one night, the Spirits told me: 'Lock up!' And they kept saying it to me over and over: 'Lock up! Lock up! Lock up!' I couldn't make any sense out of it, but they were insistent. So that's what I started doing. And don't you know that, within three days of locking everything up, some people came to rob from my house! Now, as I said, I don't have much. But at that time, I just happened to have some money there on the table. And if that money had been taken, that would have been a problem.

"Well, since the burglars couldn't steal from me, they just went on to my neighbors. There, they broke in easily and took whatever they wanted.

"So what did I learn from this? When you follow the spirits, when you listen to them, they'll protect you. They'll help you, because it's not just for them to do as you want. It is for you to listen." Then he invited anyone who wanted to share a testimony to come forward.

One woman got up and told of how her son had gotten work after listening to the spirits' messages. She had been told at a previous reunion to work with the *presidente* on a *trabajo* (spiritual work) with Santa Marta to help her son "get ahead." She testified that, in the week after the *trabajo,* her son got a call for a job interview. The week after that, he had the interview and got the job on the spot.

Another young woman came forward to testify about how she had been constantly under the influence of negative spirits. But thanks to a cleansing work prescribed by the spirits, she had been cleared of them. Now she was progressing mentally and spiritually, and was feeling peaceful. Another woman told of how her living situation had improved after she had heeded a message from the spirits.

The *presidente* then came back up to speak: "A lot of people come to me and say: 'Simon, why don't you stop that Spiritism trash? Why do you keep on with it? We have this opportunity or that, and you could be making some real money. You don't have to live like that; you can have it easier.' But my mother was an *espiritista*, and so was my father. It's in my blood. I can't stop listening to the spirits, and I am not going to.

"People tell me to cut my hair. But I keep my hair long because of the spirits. They tell me to keep it like this for my protection. Samson had long hair and that was his protection. When his hair was cut off, he lost all his strength. *Envidia* (jealousy)—that's why they want me to cut my hair. Sometimes people don't even know why they hate you for being the way you are. But it is because that's what gives you luck and they want it for themselves."

After these remarks, he pointed at a young woman and said: "Your mother-in-law can't stand you." When the woman nodded, he said: "Come to the front." And this started the message part of the service.

Eventually the *presidente* was overtaken by one of the spirits in his *cuadro*—a *muerta*, a dead woman, with whom he worked extensively. This spirit had a message for a young Mexican man, who came up to the table when he was called.

"You love drink more than anything," said one of the mediums, "and you'll die for it." The young man nodded as he walked forward and was told that he had a spirit *de causa*.

The medium then pointed at me and said: "Why don't you come here? You had many *presidentes de mesa* in your family. You were always in *sessiones* with them. You know your family has always been welcome here and that we always worked *mesas* together. *Tu atiende lo tuyo muy bien* (You attend your spirits really well), but why don't you work *mesas* with people anymore?"

I had no answer for him.

Chapter 9

ANSWERING THE CALL

The calling to be a professional *espiritista* is given by the grace of God. It is usually marked through some experience or communication from God or the spirits indicating that it is the life path individuals are meant to serve. This can often happen at a very early age. This calling also signifies a highly developed *cuadro* that has accumulated many *facultades* and plentiful *luz*. Although everyone has a *cuadro*, not all *cuadros* have accumulated the same amount of *fuerza*. Those called to be *espiritistas* have accumulated the powers to *trabajar la Obra*, to work with the spiritual plane to do the sacred work for others.

Those who answer the call to spirit go by many names—*espiritistas*, mediums, *brujos* (witches), *curanderos* (healers), and *medicos* (doctors). Each of these terms has its own connotations, both positive and negative. Professional mediums may use any of these terms to describe themselves, depending on what they want to convey. Most of these terms were used in a negative way during the various campaigns against Espiritismo, and many were used in a derogatory manner by Kardecists and others to mock believers, practitioners, and followers of Mesa Blanca. Whether or not older generations accept these terms today varies according to their upbringing.

According to my grandmother, *espiritistas* were called *curanderos* (healers) before the term *medium* came into use. Many mediums who work extensively with herbs and approach their work as a form of healing still use this term to describe themselves. These *espiritistas* are often called on to undo black magic and break curses. But the term *curandero* can be used to refer to a traditional herbal healer who does not participate in Espiritismo as well.

Among many of the older generation, the term *medico* (doctor) was also common because, in many ways, *espiritistas* were often the doctors of the people. In addition to their spiritual capacities, many mediums were gifted with the abilities to set broken bones, perform dental work, and prepare medicines for any number of ailments. Recently, we have become aware that the practices of Espiritismo can also be used to promote a healthy psychology.

One of the most popular names for an *espiritista* is *brujo*, or witch. While this may be the most controversial of the terms, it is the term most commonly applied to professional mediums in the Mesa Blanca tradition. Unfortunately, due to the Catholic background of the island and its people, many associate the term with demons, black magic, and the use of power for malign purposes. Even among practitioners, the terms *brujo* and *brujeria* are often used judgmentally to denote evil practices and black magic.

A small number of *espiritistas* and mediums who practice Mesa Blanca reject the term *brujo* because they do not practice magic and tend to see it as a misuse of their powers. In their view, spiritual abilities should only be used to align with the divine will and to engage in healing. Most practitioners, on the other hand, use the word freely. We will use the term here because it is the one that most accurately describes these practitioners.

BRUJOS

Brujos are highly developed mediums who can work magic using energy, spirits, or currents to achieve their purpose. But magic can be used to accomplish both good and evil purposes, so many fear the term. No matter what they are called, however, *brujos* never take their calling lightly. They understand that their powers come with great responsibility and they understand the ripple effects that can occur once they start using them.

Many who receive the calling to become a *brujo* run from it and resist it. But this can cause a backlash that brings suffering upon them. At times, however, the opposite happens. Novice mediums may try to work *la Obra* when, in fact, they are called to do something else. They try to force their desires, in some cases to help others, rather than discover their true spiritual purpose. This can bring its own set of headaches.

When most ordinary people need help from the spirit world, they turn to *brujos*. Moreover, mediums who are sufficiently developed to work for themselves are often directed by their own spirits to seek out other professionals when needed. This is especially common when situations involving other people are concerned. Rather than seeing it as a sign of weakness, the *viejos* praise this as a sign of strength. When mediums understand their own development, capacities, and weaknesses, this indicates that they have a strong character that radiates as a part of their light. Having the faith and courage to follow the guidance shows that they are truly walking the path and understanding the teachings.

Brujos have developed their *cuadros*, or personal spiritual power, to the point that they are able to perform *trabajos espirituales*, spiritual works. They can manipulate the powers and *corrientes* in order to make things happen. These workings are equivalent to magical spells.

Brujos perform two types of *trabajos*—*trabajos buenos* (good works) and *trabajos malos* (bad works). *Trabajos buenos* are also called *trabajos de luz* (works of light), *trabajos de sanación* (works of healing), and *trabajos de limpieza* (works of cleansing). These works are designed to remove negative energies and obstructions, to heal, or to bring about progress. *Trabajos malos*, or bad works, are works of black magic intended for malicious purposes. They seek to cause harm or damage to others through spiritual means.

This is part of the reason why people fear *brujos*. They know that *brujos* can use their powers for evil purposes. And this is why the development of character is so important in the tradition of Mesa Blanca. Using spiritual powers for negative ends causes its own set of problems. When they work with impure spirits, *brujos* leave themselves open to negative energies and spirits that can attach to them.

Brujos are able to do what they do because of the relationships and connections they have developed in their *cuadros*. For most of us, our *cuadros* are connected to us alone. Thus we have fewer connections to and faculties in the spiritual world. But *brujos* can host a greater number of connections in the spirit world and so can effect more and more change on the physical plane.

All *brujos* have the capacity to *levantar las causas*, or lift causes in order to heal or to remove bewitchments—although the type of *causas* they can handle depends on their development. Because the type of work that *brujos* can do depends totally on their *cuadros,* one of their main focuses in their process of unravelment is to develop a network of helpful relationships. A *brujo's* apprenticeship thus includes learning, not only proper self-care, but also how to work with and help others.

It's also common for a *brujo's cuadro* to agree to do only certain types of work and refuse to do others. A *brujo* I once knew used to say: "My frame will help you with your house or your job, but don't come here for no man. My *cuadro* doesn't care about that." Other *brujos* say they will only "work clean"—meaning that they won't do black magic or use their spiritual power for harming others—because their *cuadros* will make them pay for it.

When apprentice *brujos* are ready to become professionals, their *padrinos* and the spirits together give them "passage" to begin working *la Obra* and set up their healing practice. Only then can they start to use their abilities to help others. This protects both the *brujos* and the community from working with underdeveloped practitioners.

PROTECCIONES (PROTECTIONS)

Protecciones, or protections, are supernatural entities from the realm of the good spirits who have certain powers. When these entities are active in someone's *cuadro,* they lend their powers to it. There are many different *protecciones,* each of which has power in one of life's various domains. Unlike the *cuadro,* however, whose qualities and elements are born with the person, most *protecciones* can and must be acquired.

Patron saints are entities from this realm. But while most people have just this one guardian, *brujos* acquire many of them through their *desarrollo,* both in this life and in others. As they work with these entities, they become embedded in their *cuadro* and become an integrated part of it. These *protecciones* help *brujos* succeed in various areas of life, so they strive to work with them and to integrate them successfully into their *cuadros.* They then become empowered by these entities and are able to pass these powers on to those needing help.

Don Ileo was an *espiritista* who was a good friend of Doña Juana. They often visited each other, catching up on news, sharing what was going on, and just passing the hours enjoying each other's company.

Don Ileo became a *brujo* after he fell victim to negative energies and spirits at the farm where he worked. All kinds of "weird things" were happening to him and to those who worked under him. At first, he didn't really believe that malign forces could be responsible. He had never been religious or believed in "those things." But after so many strange events, there was no denying that something strange was going on. Eventually, he went to a well-known *brujo* who revealed to him what was happening and helped him acquire protections.

From that time forward, Don Ileo became interested in Espiritismo and started on the path. Since then, he has seen evidence of the spirits, of God, and of the spiritual world. While not a working medium, Don Ileo claims that his journey on the path has led him to "more peace, greater strength, and better relationships."

Each *proteccion* has very pronounced characteristics. They all have their own personalities, as well as their own likes, dislikes, and preferences. They also have characteristic attributes like colors, numbers, and implements, and they usually have rulership over a particular domain of life. Once connected to the *cuadro*, they lend their powers, weapons, and shields to it.

LOS MUERTOS (THE DEAD)

While *protecciones* lend their powers, healing, and guidance, *los muertos*, or spirits of the dead, are the ones who go out and do the work that needs to be done. They are the spirits closest to the human realm, and thus have a great deal of influence over people. Although dead, many maintain connections to the living.

There are good dead and bad dead, however. Death, contrary to popular belief, does not automatically make someone good. In fact, it is often the dead who are the cause of many misfortunes, and they are commonly called on by those doing malicious spiritual work or black magic. Cemeteries are filled with any number of *muertos* who are hungry and willing to work for a price. Since many of them are suffering, they are often willing to work in both ethical and unethical ways.

Los muertos are also often seen acting as causal spirits. They can frequently be found latching onto negativity and causing problems. They can come through causing nightmares as well as other disturbances. Sometimes a malicious *muerto* can cause sleep paralysis. Others like to haunt and scare their victims.

Some individuals are born with the spirit of a dead person that they carried forward from another lifetime. This is called a *causa* or *espiritu de existencia*—an existential causal spirit. These spirits will usually haunt and plague the person from a very young age. Many of them are very possessive and can cause their victims to become isolated by pushing others away so they can have their complete attention. Often, they are ex-lovers from another lifetime who want to keep their victims single and unable to have a romantic relationship.

Brujos have the capacity to work with all types of *muertos*, although there is usually a specific spirit with whom they work most closely. This may be a personal relative or another well-known dead person. It may also be an *emisario*—the spirit of a dead person who works alongside one of the *protecciones*.

This is one of the biggest differences between Kardecists and those who practice Mesa Blanca. Kardecists see working with the dead as holding back the spirits in their evolution. *Brujos*, on the other hand, work with the dead positively in order to help them progress more quickly.

Although *brujos* work with both the ancestors and the dead, they do not seek guidance from them. *Muertos*, just as when they were living, have their own prejudices and perceptions, some of which may not be true. Just because someone has died does not mean that they have evolved. In fact, sometimes just the opposite can happen. Rather than repenting, some become further immersed in their bad behavior.

BRUJERIA

The practice of professional *brujos* is called *brujeria*. It usually starts with a consultation, in which *brujos* investigate the client's energy system and spiritual frame using their spiritual faculties. During this consultation, they may use any number of divination tools, like tarot cards, playing cards, or shells. They may also use cigars or coffee grounds—really, the options are endless. They may also *pasar los seres* in order to pass on the spirits' messages (see chapter 7).

During these consultations, *brujos* look for *causas*, imbalances, and problems that their clients are facing. They also look for the solutions to these ills. Their job is to help their clients resolve the problems at hand and guide them toward dealing with the deeper rooted *causas* that are at play. Once they reach a proper diagnosis, they can prescribe treatment.

Brujos have many methods through which they can work. The treatments they prescribe always depend on the condition at hand. They may consist of rituals, healing ceremonies, spells, magical work, spiritual baths, *reuniones*, *veladas*, or any number of other techniques that are used to resolve a client's problems

Brujos are paid by those who come to them for help. While some reunions are held for the public, most services are conducted for personal clients, although group rituals can also be commissioned by clients for private purposes. How much *brujos* charge depends on their capacities, their experience, and their *cuadros*. Followers and practitioners of Espiritismo both know never to bargain for spiritual work, because the cost is part of the sacrifice that must be made in order for healing to take place.

Charity is one of the basic tenets of Espiritismo, but this tenet is often taken out of context and misunderstood by both followers and practitioners of the tradition. Some claim that the teachings of Allen Kardec call for the free giving of spiritual gifts. But the magical practices of *brujeria* do not come from Allen Kardec's Spiritism. In fact, Kardecist Spiritism avidly denounces such practices. *Brujeria* comes instead from native practices, and in all native traditions, the shaman was the most cherished person within the culture. Offerings had to be made to the shaman, as well as sacrifices to the dieties. As a channel for the deities, the shaman had to be taken care of in order to serve his purpose.

Thus, in Mesa Blanca, using *brujeria* and *trabajos espirituales* to get what you want does not fall into the category of charity. Working with the currents in order to manipulate life situations, heal people, or affect events is not charity. Charity is about helping people progress on their spiritual paths and develop their connections to the Divine. Charity is about encouraging faith, hope, and love.

PRUEBAS (TESTS)

The faculties and connections to the spiritual world that *brujos* enjoy do not come free. In fact, they are extremely costly—more costly than most realize or are ready to accept. Aside from the material costs incurred serving and taking care of the spirits, working with the spiritual world requires a large time commitment. Practitioners often must sacrifice a great deal of their personal time to attend to their spiritual responsibilities—to train, to learn, to develop, and also to deal with the faculties they possess.

The more powers *brujos* have, the higher the cost of their practice. In order to grow their abilities and walk the path, they are given *pruebas,* or tests, and these tests can create challenges in their lives. Many times, they must choose between the people they hold dear or the spirits and their calling. The spirits will test to whom they are more committed.

These aren't the usual run-of-the-mill types of challenges either. Many *brujos* have lived through very traumatic experiences and have had exceedingly difficult lives before discovering and responding to their calling. And although developing their faculties may resolve many of these challenges, it may also bring on its own set of problems. Since *brujos* are evolving at a faster pace, they may also be faced with more challenges in a shorter period. They may undergo even more suffering in order to understand those who will come to them for help. These experiences help them to develop compassion, wisdom, and understanding.

The work of *brujeria* takes a great toll on the body as well. Many *brujos* spend lots of time recovering from their work. And even when they aren't officially "working," they may still be receiving messages and information, and carrying the weight of those they are helping. This can put a strain on their social lives, their family connections, and their love relationships.

Brujos are also put to tests of faith by the spirits. The good spirits need to determine where to place their trust. Over time, these tests can become more and more difficult, because they are being pushed to greater and greater growth. Moreover, the spirits will, at times, throw problems and challenges into situations to help *brujos* unravel more and more.

This is why many novices reject their calling at first. Many resist because they understand all too well the costs of following it. Knowing the responsibilities that being a *brujo* brings, they run in the opposite direction. Indeed, some of the horrors that *brujos* face in order to grow would drive many people mad, make them suicidal, or turn them into criminals.

SPECIALISTS

Most *brujos* are general practitioners who can handle a great number of different situations. Many, however, also develop areas of specialization that involve additional *facultades* that become active as a result of their unravelment. Various spirits that will empower them to do the specialized work become a part of their *cuadros,* and the area of specialization becomes a refinement of their *mission divina,* their divine mission.

Some *brujos* develop the teaching faculty and are empowered by their *cuadros* to train and develop other practitioners. They take on apprentices and novices and become *padrinos* or *madrinas.* They also accept the additional responsibility of other peoples' development. Some are charged with the mission of establishing a *centro,* or spiritual healing center. They then have the responsibility of setting up and maintaining a proper space in which ceremonies can be hosted. A part of their calling is to build a sense of community.

Many *brujos,* though not all, are also *curanderos.* They may be healers or simply herbalists. Though all *brujos* generally work with herbs to some degree, not all use them for medicinal purposes. Gloria, for instance, was a well-known *santiguádora* who could heal digestive issues, mend broken bones, and bestow protection against evil and accidents. When I was a baby, my grandmother brought me to Gloria to heal a condition that kept my body from absorbing nutrients. Not only did she heal me, she reminded me every time that I saw her that "I owed her my life."

On one occasion, I witnessed Gloria perform a healing session for a woman who arrived unexpectedly. She asked the woman to lie down on the dining room table and lit a candle. Then she directed herself toward an image of the Sacred Heart of Jesus that was hanging on the wall. Taking a red bottle filled with oil and herbs, she prayed continuously as she poured oil on various parts of the woman's body. Then she put a medallion on the woman's forehead and began to rub in the oil. Occasionally, she clapped her hands and shivered as if she felt a sudden chill. She did this several times, then took a piece of cloth and rubbed off the oil. When the woman got up, she gave her a bag of herbs with some directions and sent her home.

BE CAREFUL WHAT YOU WISH FOR

Amparo's story is a tragic one. It was as if a tornado had hit her life. Not only was she severely in debt, but she had also been swindled out of all her retirement savings. Because of this and many other stresses, her marriage was on the rocks as well.

Amparo owned several empty buildings and apartments, but she couldn't get anyone to rent them, even though she had priced everything at bargain rates. She also had two other businesses, but both of them had been robbed in the same month, and the one that was left was failing. She had originally started it as a *botanica* where customers could buy spiritual supplies and she could pursue her healing practice. When that didn't work out, she added other items and made it into a thrift-store *botanica*. And when that didn't work out, she made it into a convenience-store thrift-store *botanica*. But that didn't work out either, and she couldn't even make enough to keep the lights on.

And that wasn't the end of it.

Not long ago, she had a flourishing spiritual healing practice. She worked with Santa Barbara and a *madama* curing and helping clients. She performed healings and divinations, and helped people reach all sorts of goals. Her spiritual business was going well.

But Amparo was never fully trained as an *espiritista*. She took some sporadic training here and there, but she seemed to have come by her gifts naturally. And this was one of the reasons for her downfall. At some point, she became convinced that she should start developing in the path of Cuban Santeria, a practice that shares many com-monalities with Espiritismo, but also many differences. She found a teacher, a *santero* named Luis, and started the process of initiation.

Luis was a fairly well known *santero* and he told her that she indeed had a calling to be a *santera*. Not only that, he promised that once she was initiated, her healing practice would grow beyond anything she could imag-ine—that it would take her to the "next level." Ampa-ro's husband, who was not spiritual at all, warned her about Luis. He fought with her not to pay him and not to use their retirement savings for her ceremonies. But she refused to listen and moved forward anyway.

Well, it turned out that Amparo's initiation ceremonies were done totally improperly. Ceremonies that normally lasted days were cut to a few hours. Some necessary practices and rituals were skipped altogether. Moreover, she paid more than double the normal cost for her training, completely draining her family's resources.

Amparo had been guided by impure spirits in her desire to become a *santera*. She dreamed of being a well-known and successful medium, and saw becoming a *santera* as the ultimate step that would enhance and grow her spiritual healing practice. She even imagined that great powers would be unlocked in her. But she had never been called to the practice. Her desire for fame, fortune, and a large following came from her ego, not from the spirits. Although she sincerely did want to help others, impure spirits were also present and involved in her choices.

About ten minutes into her consultation, I said: "You had a beautiful light and a strong *cuadro*. You were already connected to your *cuadro;* you already had a practice; you were doing well. So why were you initiated as a *santera*? It was this poor training and these bogus ceremonies that have trapped you in this situation."

Amparo confirmed everything, crying uncontrollably. I told her that she had to have clearing work done. Because of her *causa* of pride, however, she wanted to cleanse herself. She did not want to be cleansed by another. She was clouded by spirits of illusion, remembering when she had had the light to be able to clear others of negative spirits. This prevented her from getting the proper help. She refused to accept that she was so entangled with impure spirits that the only way for her to become clear was to receive a clearing from another.

The first major step for her was to dispose of all the spiritual items she had gotten through her botched initiation. But she had paid a lot of money for them and, although they were blocking her, she didn't want to let them go. Ultimately, she couldn't and wouldn't take this first step. She had grown so clouded by her attachment to these things that she couldn't see clearly. For her, throwing everything out meant throwing away all the money she had invested. And it also meant finally having to face the facts and fully admit to her husband that she had been taken for a ride.

Over fifteen years later, Amparo came to my house for a session. And she still had not taken that first step. As a result, her whole life was even worse than before. She had grown physically ill. But now she was willing to admit that it was her own unwillingness to let go that was at the root of the matter.

Unfortunately, stories like Amparo's are not uncommon. I have seen countless cases in which improper training and initiation practices have destroyed lives.

Chapter 10

LAS CAUSAS

Illness is a dis-ease that affects the mind or the body that may derive from the weakness or failing of a structure or from the disorder of a function. All illnesses, like everything else in creation, contain both material and spiritual elements. They are made of and possess energy.

Espiritismo sees all problems, issues, and sufferings in life as forms of illness. Bad luck, financial setbacks, and romantic issues are all sources of stress, a form of negative energy that causes pressure or tension. In fact, research shows that more than 95 percent of physical illnesses are the result of long-term stress.

Espiritistas recognize two possible sources for stress and illness, one physical (material) and the other spiritual. In cases of physical illnesses, they send their patients to a medical doctor, because these are the result of some part of the body not functioning as it should. They therefore require the attention of a doctor of the body. Espiritismo is used in conjunction with, not instead of, medical care.

If the source of an illness is spiritual, however, medical attention will not resolve it. Since the source is spiritual, the solution must be as well. But spiritual illnesses can and do create physical illnesses and symptoms, and this is part of what *espiritistas* must investigate when looking for resolutions.

All illnesses, whether originating from material or spiritual causes, have an energetic component. Therefore, *all* illnesses are a result of negative energy that has become lodged in a patient's system. This negativity, when left to fester, begins to grow, creating regular stress upon the individual that merely helps to perpetuate it. Through the action of the magnetic fluid flowing through it, it attracts spirits with the same negative vibrations.

The spiritual source of all illnesses is *causas* that are rooted in either negative energy or negative spirits. As an old *espiritista* proverb says: *No existe casualidad, solo hay causalidad* (There are no coincidences, there are only causes). There are three main sources for these forces—our innate *causas*, human magnetism, and causal spirits.

CAUSAS DE NACIMIENTO (INNATE CAUSES)

Everyone is born with what are called *causas de nacimiento,* or birth causes. These may follow us from other lifetimes, or they may be a by-product of karma, unresolved issues, and life lessons. Innate causes account for more than 70 percent of all *causas*.

These *causas* are the result of negative energies, but they are also the cause of negative attitudes, actions, and behaviors aimed at ourselves and others. Moreover, they attract the negative actions, attitudes, and behaviors of other people. They can draw bad people to you and create situations in which problems are sure to happen. This helps to create a self-supporting cycle of negativity that merely embeds negative energies deeper and deeper.

Our actions generate *causas* when we act out of hate, violence, anger, and greed. Actions require a great deal of energy. We have to think about acting, decide on an action, and finally devote energy to acting. Our actions thus have very real effects. Moreover, carrying a negative attitude toward life or a certain aspect of life is not only a condition of being; it is an action as well.

Among our actions are speech and the way that we deal with others. When we speak negatively, we give power to negativity. Cursing other people, speaking negatively about ourselves or others, and gossip are all actions that help feed negativity. Thus these actions all have the potential to attract additional *causas* back to us.

All causes create effects. It is a simple matter of action and reaction. The magic of cause and effect is called karma, which consists simply of the accumulated effects of causes, known or unknown. What most people call karma is simply the effect, the result, of some known or unknown cause or causes. Thus karma constantly changes as each effect becomes a cause in and of itself. Our *causas* are also a result of uncleared karma.

When karma is not cleared, it creates a chain and cycle of issues in our lives. Each time the karmic wheel turns, we have a chance to exercise our free will to break the cycle. Unfortunately, we often find ourselves doing the same things over and over, and the wheel just keeps turning. This is often the work of causal spirits.

Certain causes are innate to everyone and are a natural part of life itself. One of these, and perhaps the most formidable, is the *guia falsa*, the false guide. False guides seek to guide us in the wrong direction. And just as we all have a personal spiritual guide that leads us toward the good, we also all have a false guide that leads us toward actions that have karmic consequences and create avenues for the entrance of *causas*.

There are also certain experiences that leave us infested with *causas*. Major traumas often result in the attachment of causal spirits. During a trauma, we are broken open and left vulnerable, and, since trauma is inherently negative, infection is highly common. When we suffer a major trauma, illness, or negative situation, a crack in our aura occurs that allows negativity to seep in and become attached to us (see below). When this negativity accumulates or is released, it attracts negative spirits that feed off it and the suffering it has created. Once an *espiritu de causa*, a causal spirit, has attached itself to us, it remains attached so it can feed off us.

The longer we carry a trauma, the more it affects our entire life. The negative effects of the trauma seep out through us consciously and unconsciously, in our actions and in our ways of being. This helps to perpetuate the negative cycle. That is why unresolved traumas are one of the biggest sources of illness.

Many mediums naturally suffer from frequent disturbances by *causas*. Since they are sensitive to energies and spiritual influences, they are often left open to undesirable experiences with spirits. Moreover, just as mediums are open to external stresses, they are also more open to and aware of their own *causas*, although they may not know they are their own. Many people suffer through life simply because they are unaware that they have a natural capacity for mediumship. Because they are untrained, this can wreak havoc in their lives.

HUMAN MAGNETISM

We do not live in the world alone. No man is an island. The universal fluid binds and connects all things. The actions and deeds of others, including their way of being, thus can and do affect us. Likewise, we all have an energy field and exude *corrientes*. Because of this, other people, places, and things can all be the source of *causas*.

Since people naturally exude energetic fluids, they can also purposefully direct negativity toward you. This can be especially powerful when they have *causas* that match the negativity they are sending your way. Mediums and *brujos* are particularly powerful, as they are trained and have the *facultades* to direct and manipulate fluids. There are many ways that this can happen.

One thing people can do that can sour your life is to be *pendiente,* or watchful. When people are overly watchful and concerned with what you are doing, they can begin to direct their negativity and infect your actions. Not only can they direct their energy into your situation, they can also affect it with their malice. When people are watchful of your situation, unnecessary blockages and problems can occur.

In the Puerto Rican culture, it is seen as suspicious when someone asks too many questions. That is why I always teach my people: Let no one know what you are doing until it is done. In other words, only let people see the end result. It's important to keep good things a secret—especially when those things are still in progress.

Of course, sometimes it's impossible to keep people out of your business. I met one *espiritista* who was having problems building her house because of the watchfulness and envy of other people. She kept experiencing delays—repair men not showing up and projects not being completed. The watchfulness of a great number of envious neighbors and other *brujos* was slowing everything down. By the time she reached out to me, she had spent more than five years on a project that should have taken only one. The spirits had three recommendations: She needed to clear the negativity; she needed to put in protections; and she needed to put up a fence. Once we put in the proper protections and performed a clearing, she was able to get the house finished and move in within just a few short months.

Jealousy is one of the biggest problems between people. In Spanish, this is known as *envidia.* When people are jealous by nature, they are known as *envidiosos.* Jealousy most often has a direct target for the negative emotions that it pours out, and it usually hits that target unless the victim has good protections.

Jealousy can cause all sorts of problems. In the physical world, jealous people gossip behind your back, make up lies about you, and try to sabotage you in all types of ways. This can cause spiritual problems and separate you from those who would help you. Thus it can block you from being able to attain your goals.

People are often jealous without even meaning to be—even your closest relatives or friends. From an early age, we are taught to compare ourselves to others, to use others to gauge our own success. This is part of the reason that jealousy is so common.

Gossip in all its forms is destructive. When people gossip, what they say is usually not based on truth and fact. Rather it is based on assumptions and partial or incomplete information. Gossip can destroy people without them even knowing it. It directs negativity toward them, which can cause barriers to their success. Right from the start, novice mediums are warned against gossiping, because it can cause problems in their own development.

Human magnetism also works through *mal de ojo*—the evil eye. The eyes are an opening for energy. They take in energy in the form of everything we see. They also pour out energy. Every culture around the world has thus had a belief in the evil eye.

The evil eye operates when people direct their negativity to others. That negative energy is said to be directed through and passed into the eyes. Many direct negative energies in this way because they are not healed or healing. The evil eye is at work whenever hatred, envy, jealousy, or competitive thoughts are directed toward another, whether deliberately or not.

Some individuals have a naturally strong capacity to direct this energy in this way, purposefully and willfully. Others may not even realize that they are doing it. When you suddenly get jealous of a friend and direct your anger and jealousy toward that person, you are using the evil eye. This is yet another reason why being watched is considered so negative.

The evil eye most commonly affects the object or person on which it is focused. For example, when someone gives the evil eye to a person because they are "more beautiful," it can cause acne or other issues that can diminish that beauty. If directed at a specific talent, like singing or playing a sport, the victim's performance may suffer or, if the attack is bad enough, the talent may be blocked completely.

Whether you are a target of *mal de ojo*, *pendiente*, or just your own innate *causas*, these negative forces can eventually cause a breakdown.

CAUSAL SPIRITS

Spirits who are attracted to negativity become causal spirits, because they feed on negativity and carry the same *corriente*, current, as the energies on which they feed. They work to create the same type of suffering over and over so that they can continue feeding on it. These spirits come from the realm of the impure spirits. Over time, they can attach themselves like parasites, draining us of the light and creating a vicious cycle of suffering that weakens us over time. Most causal spirits do not seek to kill their victims, because then they would just have to look for another host. Instead, they prefer to feed off them slowly.

Once established, causal spirits take over more and more control of their victims' lives, eventually gaining control over their minds, their emotions, their actions, and their bodies. As time goes on, these victims can begin to break down, but the spirits who have attached themselves will stay attached for as long as they can.

Most causal spirits are *espiritus atrasados* (see chapter 4), but negativity can also attract other causal spirits that will help to support the originating *causa*. In many cases, these various secondary *causas* create problems that help to support the main *causa's* infestation. In the process, they are also fed. There are many types of supporting *causas*. Here are just a few:

- *Espiritus de confusion* (spirits of confusion) are some of the most dangerous supporting *causas*. They keep us stuck in a confused state so that we can't see or understand reason. When we fall victim to these spirits, nothing anyone can say will change what we think or believe. These spirits can also cause us to stay in a confused state, not knowing what to say or do. Spirits of confusion are usually not a main cause, but are generally attracted to and attach themselves to these causes as lesser parasites.

- *Espiritus burlones* (mocking spirits) are also particularly dangerous. They include tricksters and shapeshifters that have the capacity to deceive us into believing untruths. Because they can shapeshift, they can take the form of or pretend to be one of the higher-level good spirits. In fact, this is not uncommon among the *causas*.

- *Espiritus de arrastre* (dragging spirits) seek to drag us down throughout our lives, while *espiritus de atraso* (setback spirits) seek to make us move backward. When this happens, everything we do simply perpetuates more and more degression. No matter what we do, we always seem to go backward rather than forward.

- *Espiritus de rabia, odio, y ira* (spirits of rage, hate, and anger) inspire these same feelings in us and work to cause division and separation by creating arguments and discord among us.

- *Espiritus intranquilos* (intranquil spirits) create anxiety, instability, and compulsions in those to whom they are attached. Many of them are spirits who have died horrible deaths and are in a constant state of suffering. They are often the victims of suicide, murder, and other atrocities during life. As such, they are restless and create restlessness in their victims. Many of them cause substance addictions.

Just as the physical body requires hygiene and care, so does the spiritual body. The spiritual body encompasses the *corrientes*, the aura, and the *cuadro*. Lack of proper spiritual hygiene in any of these areas can become a personal source of *causas*.

THE AURA

The aura is like our spiritual skin. We are all exposed to negative and impure *corrientes,* just as we are exposed to viruses, bacteria, and germs. The aura, as a spiritual skin, is our first line of defense against these currents. It acts, to a certain extent, like a spiritual immune system. Imagine walking through mud, day in and day out, without ever bathing. Over time, the dirt would build up and cause a breakdown of your skin that can allow infection to enter. The same thing happens with the aura.

But the aura is also a magnet. When our *corrientes* are dirty, our auras are made of dirty fluids that attract dirty currents. This is especially important to understand. People often think of the aura solely as a protective device. But the aura can only protect against that which is opposite to its force. In other words, if your aura contains anger, it cannot protect you against it. Likewise, if your aura contains strength, then it can protect you against weakness.

Whenever we interact with other beings or share an environment with them, our energy as well as theirs is affected, just as when we shake hands we exchange germs. In a sense, when our auras interact, they are shaking hands. Generally speaking, the closer the relationship between ourselves and others the higher the risk of transference.

This is also true of those who share the same blood line. Families are connected through blood, which is part of the reason that ancestral healing is so essential in Espiritismo. In an even deeper way, sexual or romantic partners are even closer. When we interact with each other in this way, we open our auras up to a vulnerable state.

There are certain places where causal spirits may live as well. When a place is a frequent location of negativity, it creates a feeding ground for negative causes. Likewise, spirits that have been severely harmed in a certain space may become attached to it. This is the case when someone is murdered. By remaining in places that have negative energies, we can end up vulnerable to infestation. Underdeveloped mediums are particularly susceptible to this.

Cemeteries, jails, bars, places where people die, and hospitals are among those places commonly considered to be "dirty." These places typically house all types of spirits who are there both voluntarily and involuntarily. Spirits who are suffering are almost always looking for a light on which to feed.

Physical objects can also have causal spirits attached to them. This is the case of cursed objects, dolls, or artifacts. These objects can act as vessels for the negative *corrientes* and give them a place to rest and accumulate power. That is why most *espiritistas* and mediums spiritually cleanse most of their ritual items, especially spiritual tools.

When there are many people involved in an interaction, the energy of the group becomes a collective force that is stronger than that of any individual in the group and this becomes the dominating force. All members of the group will have their own reaction to the dominant force, depending on how they connect with it.

LIMPIEZA (SPIRITUAL HYGIENE)

One of the most important first steps in *espiritistas'* training is spiritual cleansing and hygiene, or *limpieza*. Through *limpieza*, the aura is cleansed. This is just a surface-level cleansing, however, and may not be enough to resolve more difficult *causas*. It may also be used to draw out *causas* that are more deeply embedded.

After *limpieza*, *espiritistas* must also learn purification, which is about cleansing the *corrientes*, the sources of the energies that are pouring out forming the aura. Purification may also be done at the same time as cleansing. Once *espiritistas* have mastered these two techniques, they can begin to unravel and deal with their own *causas de nacimiento*. Having set this foundation, they can begin to protect themselves from further illness. These practices of spiritual protection will support their spiritual immunity and help them to prevent reinfection. Spiritual cleansing, purification, and protection work together to ensure a healthy lifestyle.

SPIRITUAL POSSESSION

In Espiritismo, there are two types of spiritual possession. The first, which is desirable, occurs when a medium is mounted by a spirit. This is also called *pasar los seres,* or passing the spirits (see chapter 7). In this type of possession, the good spirits and guardians of *espiritistas* come through their bodies to help and heal. The second type of possession, which is less desireable, indicates a negative ownership of the mind, body, spirit, essence, or other part of the medium. In this type of possession, a causal spirit attaches itself to its victim and actually takes over the use of the victim's energy body.

Mesa Blanca recognizes three levels of possession. The first is the possession of the vital fluid. By taking over the vital fluid, the spirit siphons off the light and energy that the person gives off. At this level, most people do not realize what is going on. This is the most subtle form of possession and most people experience it, whether they know it or not.

The second level of possession occurs when the spirit takes over the material element, or the energy body. At this level, some people, especially those with the mediumistic faculty, can sense or even get communications from the spirit.

The final level of possession is full possession, in which the spirit effectively takes control of the vital fluid, the energy body, and finally the spirit body. For those with latent mediumship, the spirit may actually take over their physical bodies, but this is not common. More commonly, the spirit simply dominates the person's being and makes them act out.

Targets of this type of possession can end up doing things unwillingly, unknowingly, or unconsciously. Then they simply forget what they have done or totally blank out. They can also forget their good intentions to do better. Generally, all of this leads to more problems for those possessed. They often don't realize or acknowledge their part in the possession, and their refusal to accept that allows the spirit to ensure that the connection with the host stays strong.

BLACK MAGIC

Many *espiritistas* use the term *black magic* to describe the use of inferior spirits and energy for harmful ends. To say people are doing black magic can be a way of calling them out for doing something negative. These practices are not considered a part of *brujeria*, however, and within Mesa Blanca Espiritismo, it is seen as unethical to use spiritual powers to harm others.

Many mediums have the capacity to control and direct the *corrientes*. This means that they can direct negative fluids and/or spirits to another through ritual acts. If this negativity finds a place to call home or identifies breaks in the aura of a victim, it can wreak havoc. Depending on the nature of the black magic, the resulting outcome can range from small problems, to major accidents, to illness or even death.

To be *enbrujiado* means to be bewitched, and the term is usually used to describe someone who has fallen victim to a spell or has been spiritually attacked. But this is a broad term that can include many types of bewitchment. When the source of the spell is *brujeria*, its effects can be positive; when the source is black magic, its effects are usually more severe and hard-hitting.

Allie is a case in point. She had a car wreck, lost some money, and broke up with her boyfriend all in the same week. At work, things weren't any better. For a few months, she had been having problems with her coworker Sandra, who was bossy, rude, and demanding, often pushing others to do what she wanted.

It was rumored that Sandra was a *bruja*. Allie didn't really believe in witchcraft, but now she feared that she had become Sandra's favorite target. Her life was in shambles and she seemed to be the victim of constant negativity. Sandra's negative energy seemed to be everywhere—even in her home. Nyla, another coworker, had had similar issues but she seemed to be okay now, so Allie decided to talk to her about her problems.

Nyla confirmed that she had been under spiritual attack by Sandra, and that she had turned to a *brujo* for help. That *brujo* was me. When Allie came to me, I confirmed that she was, in fact, under spiritual attack and had become infested with a *causa*. We started the healing process the very next day, but it was several weeks before the negativity was completely dislodged and Allie could begin to pick up the pieces of her life.

Magic and witchcraft performed to harm other people, like that directed at Allie, can occur in many ways. There are all sorts of curses and hexes. A witch can hex part of a person's life, or attack the whole thing, or cause accidents. And there are several ways in which this malicious magic can be done.

Hexes and curses usually have a particular goal or aim. Once that goal or aim is achieved, the spell may gradually begin to wear off. This does not mean, however, that the damage that has been done disappears. Instead, victims must deal with whatever problems the black magic has caused in their lives. In severe cases, these problems may end up attracting the attachment of a *causa*.

Another method is called *enviacion,* or sending, in which an impure spirit is sent to the victim. Here, the spirit attaches itself to the person, acting just like a *causa*. This can cause endless suffering unless the spirit is removed. Over time, the spirit can slowly integrate itself into the victim's life more and more. Although these spirits may be sent to do a particular thing, they often remain attached to the victim even after the goal is met, continuing their negative impact. These spirits, like other *causas*, cause suffering in order to grow their power. Sometimes they may appear and disappear, seeming, like a cancer, to go into remission. When in remission, however, they are usually just gathering up strength to create even larger problems in their victims' lives.

Love spells are another way that these spirits create problems—sometimes for the caster as well as for the victim. Dabbling in these practices can result in causal spirits attaching to unwitting victims. Since, during magical practices, great amounts of energy are released, those who don't know how to protect their space properly can open themselves up to negative spirits who will take advantage of the situation.

UNGROUNDED FEARS

Espiritistas and mediums employ many practices that could be considered witchcraft. But they rarely perform black magic. The truth is that it depends on what side they end up on. Justice and what is seen as justice can very easily be miscalculated or misjudged. Moreover, a great deal of paranoia exists about witchcraft and black magic in Puerto Rican culture. There are many negative views held about what witchcraft is, what it's about, what it means, and what it does. The fact that the word itself can be used within Espiritismo in a negative context helps to add to these negative connotations. Since the rise of Evangelical, Protestant, and Pentecostal Christianity, this paranoia has grown even worse. In many of these sects, almost anything and everything that has to do with the material world, with nature, or with life is considered "worldly and demonic."

Due to these fears, many people come to believe that they are suffering from spiritual attacks, when in fact there is nothing of the sort happening. The supposed attackers usually have no motive and nothing to gain, yet any and every little problem, even someone stubbing a toe, has been blamed on black magic. But spiritual attacks by witchcraft are done when the attacker wants to gain something. Otherwise, why waste the time and energy?

Being paranoid about witchcraft is, in fact, a sign that the spirits of paranoia have attached to an individual and are seeking to isolate that person by causing suffering and loneliness. Because of their constant fear, these victims lose more and more of their connections to others. And because they blame everything on others, they fail to deal with the true roots of their *causas*. Remember what I said about *espiritistas* having to take personal responsibility? Well, this is one of those places where it really counts.

Fear of witchcraft also indicates a weak self-image, which is one of the main tools of the impure spirits. Many who are afflicted by it want to inflate their egos in order to feel special. If they were to face the truth—that no one really cares what they are doing—this would be a huge blow to an already weak personality. *Causas* enjoy people who have weak egos because they can cause them much suffering and so create a consistent food source.

When someone says *esa casa apesta de velas* (this house stinks of candles), it is a subtle way of saying that they suspect someone of performing black magic. I often heard this from the Christians in my family, especially when they were trying to be "nice" about it. *El tiene vasos de agua* (he has glasses of water) is another snide way to indicate that evil practices may be in play. In places, this paranoia has grown so strong that no one can even have a candle near a glass of water without arousing suspicion.

LOS ENCAUSADOS

Los encausados are individuals who are suffering from the attack of a *causa*. *Causas* work regularly to deepen and strengthen their invasion of these unfortunates. *Encausados* suffer in a variety of ways, depending on the source of the negativity. Most *causas* produce some combination of the following symptoms, as well as problems in general:

- Waking up at night

- Nightmares

- Insomnia

- Restlessness

- Chronic fatigue

- Phantom pains

- Sudden draining of energy

- Unsettling thoughts

- Lack of focus

- Anxiety, intranquility, nervousness

- Depression

- Anger issues

- Overall confusion or becoming confused easily

Some of these symptoms can indicate other problems or physical illness. Therefore, *espiritistas* always recommend proper licensed medical treatment and supervision when working with their clients. But these symptoms can indicate other spiritual conditions or changes as well.

Only a well-developed *espiritista* can diagnose the cause of these issues in each individual case. In the case of causal spirits, their character, disposition, and temperament are reflected in how they affect their victims. An alcoholic spirit may drive victims to drink. Likewise, *causas* affect the temperament, mood, and disposition of their hosts, perhaps pushing them to be depressive, moody, angry, disagreeable, or generally sour.

There are many different conditions that people can experience as the result of unresolved *causas*. Aside from the havoc they can wreak in our spiritual and physical lives, they can also create serious problems in our lifestyle, our relationships, and our ability to succeed.

- Victims who are *cruzado* (crossed up) are blocked and unable to move forward in life. Their energy is literally crossed and they become incapable of finding what they need. They may be blocked in one area of life, like work, or they may find themselves blocked in all areas.

- Victims who are *salado* (salted or salty) feel that people don't like them and may feel awkward around others. They may feel that others avoid them like the plague, and so become more sour, or "salty," themselves. They may also suffer from things regularly going sour in their relationships for no apparent reason.

- Victims who are *amarrado* (tied up) feel as if their hands are tied in a particular situation, or in life in general. They may feel totally stuck. Sometimes this condition is called being *entrapado* (entrapped), perhaps by a love spell. When this happens, victims stay with the caster of the spell, even though it isn't good for them. They may want to leave but not have the strength to do so. Or they may return with regrets after they have left.

- Victims who are *atrasado* (set back) are being backed up or slowed down. Those suffering with the spirit of backward motion find their plans being delayed or their efforts to progress thwarted. They may also find that things go back to square one over and over. This frustrates them because they know they should be farther ahead in life.

- Victims who are *arrastre* (dragged down) may feel as if a heavy weight were attached to them and keeping them down. Generally, these types of *causas* are also heavy energy feeders, meaning that they keep their victims tired all the time because they eat up so much of their energy.

- *Causas* will at times overshadow their victims, taking a form of semi-control in which they push victims around to do what they want them to do. These victims feel as is they have no other choice. These *causas* may also drive their victims to lash out at those around them simply to keep them more and more isolated.

SEEING IS BELIEVING

John could hardly get out of bed anymore. He was constantly tired and dragging himself to do what was necessary. It was as if the whole world had been painted gray. Nothing mattered and everything seemed inconsequential to him. He was simply going through the motions of life because he had to.

Two years before, John had been betrayed by his wife. Ever since then, he had been unable to move forward.

Shortly after that, he lost a good job and took a lesser job just to pay the bills. Since then, nothing had seemed to work in his favor. He didn't even have the energy or motivation to try, so he just submitted.

John was suffering from the spirit of depression, which had slowly isolated him from everything and everyone. He stopped connecting with his friends and family—even from his best friend, with whom he had been close. He tried to get out more and be more open and friendly. But things never felt right and he found himself afflicted with self-doubt, confusion, and anxiety.

John's sister, Myra, had been a client of mine for many years. Ever since his troubles began, she had tried unsuccessfully to get John to come and see me, but he always resisted and made up excuses not to come. The truth was that John was very skeptical of the "whole spiritual thing" and thought it was a waste of time. But Myra didn't give up. Finally, she was able to get John to bring her to an appointment and, since he was already there, she asked if I could squeeze him in.

As soon as John came in, the spirit of the *causa* came in with him. It was heavy and I could feel how it was holding him down, keeping him from all hope of resolution. Despite being skeptical, John admitted he was amazed that I could see all that I did. I delivered many *videncias* to him about which only he knew. So, although still unsure whether it would work or not, he agreed to give the healing work a shot. I worked with John over a period of three months. We resolved the *causa*, and John experienced a great number of positive changes in his life.

The resolution of this *causa* encouraged John to walk the path of his spiritual life. This experience opened him up to the fact that there was more at play in the world than what his eyes could see. During his healing work, John himself had various spiritual experiences, even seeing the spirits at times.

Chapter 11

SPIRITUAL HEALING

Espiritistas work *causas* by healing both the *causa* and the *encausado*. This process is known as *levantando las causas*, or lifting the causes. It is also known as *sanación,* or healing. Depending on the causes and the depth at which they have possessed and attached to the individual, they are dealt with in various ways.

Not everyone has the *cuadro* to be able to lift *causas*. That is usually left to the work of *brujos* and mediums. Depending on their capabilities and the strength of the *causas, brujos* may be able to handle them in private rituals with clients. Cases in which the *causas* are particularly strong or stubborn may require *veladas*. Mediums who are not *brujos* can sometimes work collectively during *veladas* to remove *causas,* the collective force gathered from the group giving them the ability to overpower the causal spirits.

The process of lifting causes consists of three steps and may occur in one or multiple sessions. The first step, called investigation, is to find out the root of the *causa* through consultation with the medium or spirits. This is the most important step, because it ultimately determines the proper treatment. This investigation can take place during private consultation with a *brujo*, in a session, or in a *velada*.

If the *causa* is determined to be coming from other people via *brujeria* or human magnetism, the *espiritista* may prescribe a nullification or counterattack. For this, the victim will most often be directed to work with a *brujo* privately. If the *causa* is determined to be a spirit, a *levantamiento* is performed by a professional medium and assistants in a private setting or during a *velada*. During this process, the medium opens a dialogue between the causal spirit and the *encausado*.

This conversation can happen in one of two ways. In one method, the causal spirit takes possession of the medium and speaks to the person directly. In the other, the medium's good spirits come through and speak on behalf of the *causa*. During this conversation, the spirit reveals itself and its reason for being attached, and describes what it has caused. This process is a part of the healing and closure for both the spirit and the victim. The connection with the causal spirit represents an agreement between the two parties. To a certain degree, people can often become attached to their *causas*, even though they see the harm that they cause. This conversation also reveals what is needed for the spirit to let go of the person. The spirit may also make certain requests that the medium must negotiate, and corrective actions and measures may be required of the *encausado*.

Once closure has been reached, the actual lifting of the causal spirit begins. During this step, the spirit is encouraged and led into the *escuela espiritual*, or spiritual school. This is also called being led into the light. Understanding that all spirits are in the process of development, *espiritistas* see that most causal spirits are misguided, suffering, and confused, and thus in need of elevation. By going to the spiritual school, the spirit learns to do better and to continue on the path of progress. In *veladas* or group rituals, this will often be accomplished through the collective prayer of the congregation, who are asked to direct their prayers and thoughts toward the spirit's upliftment. In private settings, the medium may use passes, or various *trabajos* may be prescribed or performed.

In cases where one of the *guias* is present, the guide may tell people to perform certain actions in order to assist. Or the guide may simply carry the spirit away into the light.

When the source of the cause is discovered to be underdeveloped mediumship, the only solution is to begin the process of *desarrollo*. Underdeveloped mediumship almost always has the side effect of attracting many causal spirits. In this case, the person may be directed to begin apprenticeship and to attend regular *sessiones*. As novices develop, the causal spirits will begin to drop away.

Once the *causa* has been lifted, the process of *sanación* can begin. During this process, the person undergoes a healing to the damaged system that allowed the *causa* to become lodged in the first place. This is the equivalent of sealing a wound and applying medicine for it to heal. Just as in any healing process, this is usually the step that takes the longest.

PASSES

Passes are one of the primary methods that mediums use to direct *la luz* and other currents. They are used by *espiritistas* to clear energy, remove spirits and energy, heal, call in their guides, and more. Passes are also known as *despojandose*, or self-cleansing. Passes clear and cleanse the aura of collected negative energies. They can also serve to open the aura up so the energy system can be worked on. Using passes, mediums can channel the fluids of the spirits and use them for various purposes.

Passes are performed by passing the hands over the body in sweeping motions, usually hovering but not physically touching. Mediums may rub their hands with Florida Water or some other spiritual cologne as they do this. Throughout the process, they may *santiguar* (bless by drawing the sign of the cross) or make any number of other movements to direct the fluids. Passes are usually accompanied by deep prayer to reinforce and strengthen the currents.

When removing negative energy or spirits, *espiritistas* grab onto it or collect it into closed fists and then dump it into the *fuente*, which acts like a sponge to absorb all the negativity. In the case of spirits, the *fuente* serves to conduct the entities to the proper spiritual realms.

Passes may also be performed with various items. Sometimes *barridas,* or sweepings, are done by passing a bundle of herbs along the body of the patient in various directions depending on the purpose of the treatment. The medium may also tap or lightly beat various parts of the body. Passes employ magnetism to channel the forces of the higher spirits so mediums can pass a greater amount of light through their bodies to the patient.

THE POWER OF WATER

Water is essential for life. It represents the universal fluid. In fact, all drinking water has been recycled. The water you are drinking now is the same water that was drunk by your ancestors, purified through nature.

Research has shown that water receives and holds energetic imprints or patterns. It is a conduit for energies—for instance, for electricity, which is merely another form of *la luz*. As such, it acts as a conduit for the light and the spiritual energies with which *espiritistas* work. Water is thus a major tool in Espiritismo and is used in most rituals.

Moreover, water can be magnetized. When it is magnetized, it is impregnated with specific currents and those currents can be used to cure or to curse. Many *brujos* have become famous for their cures using magnetized water.

BLESSINGS AND PRAYER

Santiguar means to bless, often by making the sign of the cross. *Ensalmar* refers to healing through prayer. Using the energies generated by blessings and prayers, *brujos* heal people. These energies can also be used as a means of protection.

When *brujos* pray, their prayers can be used in either a negative or a positive way. In the process of prayer, currents are directed at a person through the reciting of particular words. The nature of the prayers determines the magical effects they will have on those who are targeted. Prayers are often used in conjunction with candles.

The Bible—particularly the Book of Psalms—is a powerful tool in the hands of *espiritistas*. In fact, the word *ensalmar* comes from the name of this book. Each psalm has its corresponding aims and anyone who knows how to use them can perform this type of magic easily. Even people who identify as Chrisitans use the psalms in this way. That is why you often find the Bible among the books *brujos* keep—because it is known to be a powerful book of magic. But there are also other prayers found in other books commonly used by *espiritistas*. In the hands of *brujos*, these prayers act like spells and are particularly powerful. Thus they are an important component of many *trabajos*.

TRANSFERRING THE *CUADRO*

Brujos can transfer their *cuadros* temporarily to another person in order to elevate, heal, or help. This temporary transfer can also cleanse the recipient of negative influences and remove blockages. This can be done in person by passing the hands over the body, or with certain other movements and gestures. Moreover, the transfer can be done regardless of the physical distance between the medium and the target.

Brujos can also transfer or send a particular protection or court of guides. This may be done to treat issues or to lend the person abilities that they otherwise lack. These protections come with immense force, because they carry the strength of the practitioner's *cuadro*. After a short time, the *cuadro* simply returns to its owner. It is important to note, however, that, even though the *cuadro* has been transferred, the *brujo* is not without protection. Some part of the *cuadro* always remains behind with its owner.

In the past, this was one of the main forms of activating a student's spiritual abilities. In fact, simply spending time with someone whose *cuadro* is highly developed can uplift less-developed *cuadros*. Likewise, transferring the *cuadro* has the effect of activating lights or spiritual abilities in students.

There is an unqualified fear among some untrained *espiritistas* that, if they transfer their *cuadro*, they may not get it back. They also fear that they may be left without protection while the *cuadro* is away. This is entirely untrue, because the *cuadro* always returns to its owner without issue when the owner is clean, clear, and on track. And while the *cuadro* is away, its owner is never left without protection.

STRONG MEDICINE

The sun had barely risen when I was awakened by Tia Berta to have a morning coffee and get started with the day. I couldn't believe we were up so early. I got my bearings and dragged myself to the little table, where I found a cup of nice hot coffee with a piece of Puerto Rican baked bread balanced on the rim. After taking a tiny sip, I cleared my throat and asked Berta for the sugar. The coffee was good, but extraordinarily strong and bitter. I was used to having my morning beverage taste more like milk with a dash of coffee. Berta laughed and gave me a devilish grin. *At least someone is amused,* I thought, slightly irritated.

Berta was my *madrina's* sister and a professional medium. She was a short stout woman with a strong frame and an equally strong presence who could almost always be found at home wearing a housecoat and busy with some task. We had arrived at her home the night before because my *madrina* thought it would be a good idea for me to spend a day learning from her.

"We've got a full day," Berta said as she reached for the sugar. "Today we are going to work *la Obra* and tonight we will attend a session." As a professional medium with a well-established practice, Berta was often invited to sessions to "work *la mesa.*"

"We are going to go get the herbs when you finish there, so put on your shoes," she said as she walked off into her own room.

In the yard, Berta kept a small garden that was filled with all the herbs she used in her work, as well as vegetables that she grew for consumption—rue, basil, thyme, mint, *brazo fuerte*, *higuerta*, rosemary, oregano, fresh peppers, and tomatoes. Toward the back, there were mangos, plantains, bananas, and *carambola,* all growing wild. In fact, her garden was a tropical paradise.

We picked some rue, basil, and rosemary, and then headed to the other side of the garden to gather some orange leaves. On our way back to the house, we picked fresh white wildflowers that would be used to refresh the blessed water and placed on the *mesa espiritual* that Berta had set up in a small back room off the kitchen. This room, less than ten feet square, was known as "the coffee room," and had apparently at one time been the room in which coffee beans were roasted and ground. According to Berta, every house used to have one.

Berta's altar room was vastly different from anything I had seen before. Other than a narrow stream of light that came in through the open kitchen door behind us, the only light in the room came from a glass-encased white candle that was burning on top of a long stone. The decorations in the room were very sparse. There was a huge stone laid against the longest wall that was covered in patches of moss and candle wax. This served as the central altar. In front of the stone was a large blue drum, the kind used to ship things overseas. This was filled with water that had herbs and flowers floating in it. It smelled divine.

Four dresses hung on the four walls of the room, each one with a candle sitting on the floor in front of it.

Countless cigar butts sat next to each of the candles. Four large orchids hung in the four corners of the room, all in full bloom. Two old dining room chairs and a rocking chair completed the furnishings.

"*Yo trabajo con los Indios* (I work with the Indians)," Berta exclaimed as I took in the contents of the room. Then everything we had collected was placed directly on one side of the large stone altar. There, she lit a small white candle and recited the Our Father several times. She lit a cigar and, as she puffed away intently, she began a long prayer and invocation. As she did so, she blew cigar smoke all over the items. Here's part of her prayer:

I invoke, call, and conjure the Virgin of Light to amplify the light and draw it to the spirit of the seven winds to blow away negativity, confusion, and jealousy. With the smoke of this cigar, I invoke the Indian of Peace to bring peace to their house, their hearts, their souls, and their lives. To the blessed and holy Saint Claire, clear the roads and minds.

Berta continued praying until she had finished her cigar, after which she placed the butt onto a corner of the stone altar. Appearing somewhat dazed, she got up and rubbed her hands with Florida Water, then sat back in one of the chairs.

The flowers and a bit of one of the herbs we had gathered were placed in the blue shipping drum that sat in front of the stone. Then the drum was refilled with water and a bottle of Florida Water was emptied into it. As Berta prayed over the drum, she lit a white candle. Then her whole body started to shake as if she had received an electrical shock. She dropped the candle into the water and grabbed the side of the drum.

Regaining her footing, she filled a large can with water from the drum, placed the other herbs we had gathered in it, and sat it on the stone altar. She placed a fresh white candle on the altar along with two new cigars, then plopped herself down in her rocking chair with a deep sigh. Now we were ready to begin; all we had to do was sit and wait.

As I sat there, Berta stared at me with a deep penetrating gaze, unblinking and motionless. I wondered what she was thinking and what we were going to do next. It felt as if time stood still in that room, as if we were in a world where time never existed. I'm not sure if we were there for a minute or an hour—that was the magic of the room. It seemed as if we were sitting there forever, and yet I don't think that much time had passed at all.

A loud knock broke the silence. Berta simply pointed to the door, motioning me to bring the person in. My body felt heavy as I got up, as if I had just woken up from a deep sleep. I swung open the door to find Mercedes standing there.

Mercedes was a woman in her late thirties with long dark hair that she always kept pulled back in a ponytail. She was very physically fit and had an extremely high and excitable energy that oozed out of every ounce of her being. She was very loud as well, and half the time I wondered whether she was just talking or screaming. She was one of Berta's very few apprentices. Berta no longer took on new students, but Mercedes had been learning from her for more than ten years and was probably one of her closest friends.

Without waiting for a sign from Berta, Mercedes immediately set to work in the kitchen, starting a fresh pot of coffee and cutting the *pan de agua* she had brought with her, setting the slices of bread on a tray in a spiral pyramid. Then she prepared a fresh juice from a mixture of oranges, lemons, and limes. I helped her take all this over to a small patio-like area just outside the kitchen where Berta's patients sat and conversed while waiting to be seen. On wet days, they were ushered into the living room to wait their turn. On a little table between the chairs sat a box of dominoes that people, especially the men, used to pass the time while children played tag and chased a ball around the yard.

You could tell that those who came to see Berta felt relaxed and at ease when they were there. In fact, many came on a regular basis just to sit and hang out on days when Berta was not giving treatments. Berta almost always had company.

After setting everything up, we went back into the altar room to find Berta exactly as we had left her—staring off into the distance, her eyes conveying that, at least mentally, she was in a faraway place and time. She didn't even seem to notice when we entered. When she finally did notice us, her face gleamed with a wide bright smile.

"*Ay Mercedes*," she exclaimed as she got up to greet her with a traditional kiss on the cheek and a strong hug. "Let's go to the patio."

There we sat as the warm breeze caressed us. Mercedes and Berta caught up on the latest neighborhood news, laughing and giggling like schoolgirls. The sun continued to grow warmer and warmer as we absorbed its precious rays. Sitting there in pure peace and serenity, problems didn't exist. Nothing was ever rushed here, and the relaxed atmosphere was like being on vacation all the time.

As I think back on it, I realize that there were no cell phones at the time, or at least they were not common. Nor did Berta have a TV. No Internet; no Wi-Fi. The only electronic connection to the outside world was a small radio and a phone with a long coiled cord that attached to the base of its receiver. Life there was simple and Berta made sure to keep it that way.

We sat there for quite some time before Nina arrived, all flustered and out of breath and apologizing for being late. But we were on Puerto Rican time, so it was expected and no one cared. Berta waved her hand and made a face that conveyed her utter lack of concern for Nina's tardiness.

Nina had just started on the spiritual path. She had problems with being unemployed and had finally sought Berta's help. After her first visit, she had succeeded in getting a job. Once she got the job, she came back to thank Berta and to consult her again. In that consultation, Nina was informed that she needed to unravel herself spiritually. This was Nina's third visit to Berta.

Slowly, we all got up and Berta led the way into the altar room. As we were walking through the door, it came to me that Nina was having a problem with her children. After we were seated, Berta lit a match and brought one of the cigars to her lips. Then she mumbled a short prayer and lit the cigar with one long draw.

She looked at Nina and said: "Your children have been all over the place. You've been yelling and screaming a lot."

Nina nodded, confirming the message.

"You've been feeling worn down and out. Yes, they are irritating you, but you are also just irritated."

Again, Nina confirmed.

Berta continued, saying that Nina was starting to experience pain in her legs and problems breathing. The pain suddenly appeared and then just as suddenly disappeared. She felt as if she didn't know where to go or what to do, not just with the pains but with her children as well.

Berta then told Nina that she would *despojarla,* or cleanse her. She told her to lie down on the long stone altar, then lit another cigar and began a prayer to Nina's holy guardian angel. After a long litany of prayer, she invoked her *cuadro espiritual*, asking them to come to her aid.

Laying the cigar down on one end of the stone, Berta took a handful of herbs and passed them over Nina's body. She passed her empty hand first, slowly gathering it from an open palm into a fist, and then passed the hand that held the herbs. Finally, she tapped her fist over the drum of water and opened her hand.

Berta worked on various areas of Nina's body over and over, blowing air on her at various points to dispel the negative energy. All the while, she talked to and directed the various spiritual entities present to help her in her healing.

Eventually Berta's main guide, Tupate, appeared to continue the healing work. Working briskly, he spoke in a deep voice with an accent. He smoked the cigar and blew huge plumes of smoke into different parts of Nina's body. Using both hands together, he scooped up negative energies and dumped them into the blue drum. When he had finished, Berta regained herself and began to sprinkle the blessed waters onto Nina.

Chapter 12

GETTING STARTED
ON THE PATH

The first step to getting started on the path of Espiritismo is to find an *espiritista* whose *cuadro* has agreed to take you on as an apprentice. This is very necessary in the spiritual realm because of the many dangers that exist. When *espiritistas* first start to develop, their powers are weak and unfocused, and this can cause them a host of issues. *Espiritistas* cannot simply declare themselves working mediums; only the elders and the spirits, through the elders, can grant that capacity.

The United States is the land of "do it yourself," and this has created a crisis in the world of spirituality. Many people without proper training are taking on work for others, often leaving them more troubled than when they started. Even worse, some of these *espiritistas* are presuming to teach others and claiming to be godparents or mentors. This is like the blind leading the blind, and is totally out of alignment with the tenets of Espiritismo. In fact, it is the very contradiction of it.

The spirits can and do punish those who work for others without the proper development and permissions. Just because you can do something, does not mean you should. You cannot say you respect the spirits, the tradition, or the powers of *espiritistas* if you do not follow the rules. You can't say you are a doctor just because you have read a few medical books,

In the tradition, most novices attend dozens of *veladas* before ever attempting to do any work at all—not even setting up their own altars—because this allows for the clearance of many energies that could work to confuse them. Only under the careful guidance of their *padrinos* can novices learn to discern between the various energies coming toward them. In the beginning, apprentices are not even allowed to share their visions, as they haven't yet developed their faculty of discernment. That is why elders never allow those starting on the path to do psychic readings, divinations, or investigations. Rather, apprentices are expected to sit, observe, and learn over time how to do these things. Only when the time is right are they asked to share their *videncias* during *veladas*.

Many *espiritistas* who are called to do *la Obra* find that they can see, hear, and receive messages from the spirits before they have completed their proper development on the path. This often leads to the misguided belief that they are ready to work for others. But when they attempt to do this prematurely, they often attract all sorts of *causas* and negative energies onto themselves. Time and time again, I have seen the lives of inexperienced *espiritistas* fall into complete shambles because they have done work for others before they were ready. Remember Amparo's sad story.

This was the case with Lina, who came to me because she was feeling mentally, emotionally, and spiritually exhausted. She was also starting to experience several health issues and her finances were in shambles. Lina was a natural medium who had been convinced by several of her non-mediumistic relatives to set up a spiritual center. But Lina had never trained with any *espiritista*. She had grown up attending *reuniones* with her parents and she thought that "it wasn't that hard to do." Unfortunately for poor Lina, she had no idea how much goes into working with the invisible realms.

At first, Lina loved her work. She held *reuniones* as best as she could and found that she could deliver messages from the spirits with some accuracy. She did cleansings and *revoccaciones,* returning negativity to the sender, and her clients reported feeling better. In fact, she could see that her work was helping them and this gave her more confidence. But by the time she came to me, Lina was in need of a deep cleansing and some healing work herself.

In our session, the spirits told her that she needed to shut down her spiritual center and work on getting some training and developing her faculties. The center need not be closed forever, just until she was properly prepared to work for others. They warned that, if she continued to run the center, she would experience problems not only with her health, but also in her marriage, with her children, and, in time, with members of the center.

Lina received the cleansing and the healing prescribed for her, but she was unwilling to close down the center or to get training. She didn't want to do the foundational work and healing required to become a true *espiritista*. She had grown to enjoy all the praise and attention she got from running the center. She wasn't acting out of love, but rather for her own self-aggrandizement. By doing so, she was disrespecting the tradition and the spirits, and working against the very tenets she claimed to follow. In fact, she was simply transferring her clients' issues onto herself. Once she was cleansed and healed of the negativity she had attracted to herself from others, many of the people she had previously "helped" began to experience all the same issues she was supposed to have resolved.

About a year later, I saw Lina again and she was in an even worse state. She was feeling more drained than before and her health issues had worsened. She had suffered several major financial losses and her husband was in the process of divorcing her. The center had been under a number of spiritual attacks and there were conflicts among its members. Many of the center's members had left and the center was no longer able to pay for itself, much less anyone working in it.

ALTARS

One thing that you can do on your own, however, is to set up an altar, a *mesa espiritual,* although it is preferable to have a proper guide to help you. This is the place from which you serve the Divine, and connect with your *luz* and your *cuadro*. It is also the place where you learn to communicate with your spirits and open your spiritual faculties so you can learn discernment.

At its most basic, an altar consists of a small table or the top of a dresser that is covered with a pure white cloth. It usually holds a large bowl or glass of water at the center—the *fuente*—as well as a white candle, a Bible, and other prayer books. It may also hold flowers, an incense burner, and a rosary. Many people keep pictures of deceased relatives on or around the altar, but these should never be mixed with photos of living persons.

The altar may also contain bottles of Florida Water and other spiritual colognes, known as *alcoholados*. These are used to perfume the altar as well as the *espiritista*. Be careful when using Florida Water or any other type of *alcoholado*, however, because they are highly flammable. Keep them away from candles and fire, and make sure not to sprinkle them on candles or near fire accidentally.

Divination tools like tarot cards, pendulums, and other aids in spirit communication can also be kept on the altar. At first, however, most recommend that novices not use such tools because they can become a crutch and a distraction from the development of their faculties. Tools should only add to your faculties, not replace them.

Once you have set up your altar, you should attend to it for at least fifteen to twenty minutes a day for at least ninety days. During this time, you begin to build your connection to God and the light. When you do this, lightly focus on the *fuente* (see below) while you sit and relax as much as possible.

Start by lighting a white candle on the table and reciting any of the following prayers:

- The Our Father

- The Hail Mary

- The Glory Be

- The Opening Prayer

- The Medium's Prayer

- The Prayer to the Spirit Guides

- The Prayer of the Shipwrecked

Once you have said the prayers, begin to focus lightly on the *fuente*.

Espiritistas and mediums keep anywhere from one to several altars where they focus on their religious rituals. In the past, these were always built on four-legged tables, but today they are also built on shelves and in book cabinets. These altars can be set up anywhere in the house, but are often placed in the corners of rooms or in closets. When possible, mediums avoid placing altars in bedrooms because of the nudity and sexual activity that take place there.

The word *altar* is often used to refer, not just to the table itself, but to the whole room in which it is kept. Some *brujos* also refer to this as a *santuario,* or sanctuary. Not all *brujos* have a whole room dedicated to the work, however, and many set up their altars in dining rooms, living rooms, and other spaces.

Different altars and setups hold different purposes or are dedicated to different guides. Regardless of their purpose, however, altars are considered foundational to the practice and are one of the most important tools *espiritistas* use to develop their faculties. In fact, a simple altar setup is considered all that is necessary for the work to be performed.

Most practitioners keep a personal altar table dedicated to their *cuadro* that is designed according to the instructions of their *guias espirituales.* This altar reflects their spiritual frame and no two are ever quite the same, although they all follow some basic rules. They usually include a *fuente,* at least one candle, various prayer books, and perhaps a bell or a rosary. These personal altars can be decorated in various colors and the *espiritistas's* patron saint is usually found sitting in some central position, along with his or her *guia principal.*

Since *brujos* often have many spirits working within their *cuadros*, it is not uncommon for their altars to hold many spirits. On some altars, these are arranged according to their courts; on others, they are mixed together. Some contain only saints and some only the patron saint. Some are simple and spare, while others spill over with statues lined up like a spiritual army ready to do battle. (Remember Doña Ana's impressive display.) Some contain no statues at all, but are surrounded by images of spirits attached to the walls. Some altars are small; some are huge. But no matter how they are set up, they are always intensely powerful.

Another quite common type of altar in Espiritismo is the *boveda*. These altars entered the tradition with the influence of Cuban Espiritismo, Cruzado, and Santeria. *Bovedas* are altars to the dead and to the guides. Unlike *mesas espirituales*, which are altars to all the *espiritista's* spirits, *bovedas* are only used for certain classes of spirits. Likewise, the rules for using *bovedas* differ from those used by most Mesa Blanca practitioners.

Bovedas feature a large central fountain that holds a crucifix to represent God. The fountain is surrounded by a number of other glasses, usually seven or nine. Each of these glasses is dedicated to a spiritual guide or an ancestor, or to a group of spirits.

An important tenet of Espiritismo is that the power of the work resides in practitioners and their *cuadros,* not in the items and tools they use. When setting up altars, however, people sometimes assume that more "stuff" means more power. This was the case with Yiselda, who had one of the loveliest altars I had ever seen. More than five dozen saints and statues of all types of guides adorned it and it was covered with yards of bright satin cloths in all colors of the rainbow, dozens of flickering candles, and plates of various types. But something essential, something deeper, was missing.

When Yiselda consulted my *madrina* about the illnesses, problems, and losses she was experiencing, she was told: "*Esa mesa está vacía* (This table is empty). *Tu no tiene la fuerza para la Obra y como no tiene te sigue jodiendo* (You don't have the force to do spiritual work and since you don't have it you keep hurting yourself)." Although Yiselda really wanted to help others spiritually, that was not her purpose or calling. She hadn't been given the grace. Her purpose was to help people in a different way. And when you do work that's not right for you, you suffer.

Yiselda's is not the only empty altar I have ever seen. Some I have seen were set up in ignorance. Some were set up deliberately by unethical practitioners to misguide people. Others were rendered empty through lack of attendance. In most cases, they were the result of a lack of proper development on the part of their owners that kept them from seeing what was really going on.

FUENTES (FOUNTAINS)

Fuentes, or fountains, act as conductors for *la luz* and the spiritual fluids. They deliver the messages of the spirits in various ways. Sometimes we say *la fuente habla,* or the fountain speaks. As mediums develop their faculties, however, this happens less and less, because messages can be passed clearly to them. Sometimes bubbles show up in the fountain to indicate the strong presence of spiritual fluids and spirits. If no bubbles appear, however, this does not necessarily mean that the spirits are not present. Sometimes the water in a fountain can turn murky and gray—sometimes in just a few days. This happens when it has collected negative energies and become polluted. Sometimes bugs or flies may die in the water of the fountain, indicating the strong presence of enemies. When this happens, appropriate work must be done to clear it.

Fountains should be cleaned once a week, unless they get severely dirty before that. Professional mediums may have to clean their *fuentes* more often because they come in regular contact with others, whose negative energies may dirty the waters more quickly. Whenever a fountain becomes polluted, it should be cleaned right away. The waters of the fountain should be poured out onto the ground; they should never be flushed or poured down the sink, as this can and does cause issues with the pipes over time.

Once the water has been emptied, you can wash the fountain with soap and water just as you would any other dish. If it was polluted or has collected bugs, fill it with water after washing it and pour in three dashes of Florida Water. Let it sit on the altar for three days, then dump it out again, rewash it, and put it back on the altar filled with clean fresh water.

It is important to set up and maintain your fountain properly. This is not the time to start doing magical works, or psychic readings and the like. This is the time to settle in and build the foundations of your practice. If you skip over these important steps, it will be very noticeable to experienced *espiritistas*.

BUILDING A FOUNDATION

People beginning on a spiritual path are often excited "to get to the good part." This is very understandable, especially for those who have been trying to figure things out on their own. If you have just encountered the spiritual realm, or even if you've been involved for some time, it can be an extremely exciting and wonderous world that contains many new and interesting things to learn and explore. But you will have plenty of time to get to that. And you can't build your faculties or develop your abilities without a good foundation.

Without a proper foundation, spiritual practices usually cause more issues and problems than they correct. Working with spirits or magic before you are ready creates karma and effects that you may not be ready to deal with. This can often become a source of *causas* and create more problems than you had when you started. In fact, it often creates *causas* that can take years to unravel and work through, preventing you from achieving success. The way to avoid this is simple: Get a mentor and don't start without a proper foundation.

When you begin your apprenticeship, you may begin to be aware of messages coming to you. You may even be able to write them down. But do not believe them all and don't act on them. During this time, you will be undergoing a lot of cleansing and clearing, and these "messages" may not be messages at all, but rather the clearing out of old mixed-up energies you have been carrying around with you. Spirit communication may come from *causas,* and people often forget that many *causas* are incredibly wise and can tell you things that are true. But some are not.

If you do receive messages and write them down, just put them aside. You can always review them later to see if they contain anything pertinent. If you are already a practicing spiritualist, they may help you to get clear on some things. You can underline or highlight anything that seems to be a spirit message to you. Then, when you review them later, you can get a clearer picture of yourself.

Prayer and sharpening of your will are two important elements in becoming a great *espiritista.* If you cannot commit to the ninety-day period required to build a strong foundation without distracting yourself in other spiritual activities, you should really look at your commitment toward development. Ninety days is not a long time to devote to something you will likely be doing for the rest of your life.

Once you have completed ninety days of training and have begun to develop a connection with *la luz,* you can begin to serve your guardian angel. Guardian angels work on behalf of the divine will, and it is a misunderstanding to think that they are only there to protect you from life's difficulties. In fact, when in proper alignment, they provide challenges for the growth and development of your soul. They can, however, as the name indicates, defend and guard you from immediate danger.

BASIC TRAINING

By this point in your training, you have probably found yourself an appropriate material guide, or mentor, who will perform an *investigacion*, or investigation of your spiritual frame. In this consultation, your mentor will tell you what you must do in order to develop your gifts and your *cuadro*. Often, although not always, you may also be introduced to some of the spirits who are a part of your frame.

Next, you will begin to develop *la luz* and your power. If your *padrino* or *madrina*, your godparent, also runs a *centro*, he or she may require that you attend any *reuniones* or *Misas* performed there. Throughout the course of your training, you will be taught how to discern the various currents and shown how to clean *la casilla*, or the house of the spirits, so that only the highest and purest spirits will come through.

As you grow and unravel, your *facultades,* or spiritual faculties, will begin to manifest. Mediums begin to develop their faculties, and to discover and illuminate new ones, through the process of *desarrollo,* or unraveling, which causes the light to develop. Although at this point, some mediums may be receiving messages, they are advised not to follow through on them, but rather to write them down so they can be checked by the *padrino* to determine which ones come from good spirits and which ones come from dark spirits. This also helps mediums develop their power to discern between different fluids.

During your training, your *padrino* will also administer passes or work on you spiritually, healing and resolving blockages between you and *la luz*. When your *cuadro* is strong enough, the process of removing and lifting *las causas* begins. This can only happen after all blockages to the light have been removed because, without the light, new mediums don't have the strength to fully resolve *causas*.

Being free of *causas* is most essential to mediums. When mediums carry unresolved *causas*, the messages they receive will be contaminated. This is one of the main problems that underdeveloped and untrained mediums face. At the start of their training, novice mediums always need the help of their mentors to remove *causas*, because this requires a strong light—something they are still developing. Once their light has developed to a certain degree, however, they can cast off many of their own *causas*.

Once novices are free of *causas*, they can begin to develop connection to and communication with the spirits in their *cuadro*. By this point, they have learned how to develop the light, how to discern between fluids, and how to keep their *casillas* clean. They have also learned how to clear themselves of *causas* and how to do passes on themselves. They have set up their altars and work with them frequently.

If they haven't already done so, they are ready to set up their *mesas espirituales*, which are dedicated to the main spirits in their *cuadro*. Their mentors will help them by transferring their own *cuadros* and through *levantamientos*, or the strengthening and lifting of spirits. Novices may also have *veladas de desenvolvimiento* performed—special ceremonies that are aimed at developing their *cuadros*.

PRAYER

There are few tools more powerful than prayer. Prayer represents a sincere focus to connect with God and the divine forces. Through it, we can reach many of the answers we seek. But to do so, we must ask the right questions. Asking the wrong questions gets us either no answers or the wrong answers, and this can leave us stuck and confused. When the *viejos* tell us to "sit and talk to the spirits," they are telling us to go and pray.

God doesn't fix what he gave us the sense to fix ourselves. God doesn't answer when we could have found the answer ourselves. God doesn't do for us what he gave us the power to do for ourselves. Rather, God is for what we *can't* do. This is something I tell my god-children and my clients all the time. Do not expect to be given easy answers where due diligence, research, learning, training, or a bit of common sense can get them for you. Do not expect to pray and receive that which can be earned by hard work.

When you pray, you must offer up your prayers in honesty, sincerity, and truth. You must be connected. You cannot just spew out a bunch of empty words and expect a response. Prayer must come from the deepest part of your heart.

Lo santos no oyen, sienten (The saints don't listen, they feel). This saying is common in my family. It means that the spirits respond to honesty, passion, and your heart—your truest heart—more than any vocalized words. They do not listen to your prayers; they feel them. An *espiritista* once told me: *Los seres comen corazones* (The spirits eat hearts). They respond to your sincerity, your heart's "feltness." They want to help, but they need authenticity in order to respond.

When I was young, whenever I had a question about a spiritual matter I was told: *Ve al altar y ore* (Go to the altar and pray). During my training, I was told: "Once you have an answer, or what you believe is the answer, come with your question and your answer. Then we will show you." I was expected to attempt to find the answer on my own, then seek out the elders to either confirm or reject it. This was how they taught me.

And this lesson is very important for novice *espiritistas*. So many today are accustomed to being handed things easily or being given the answer right away. But novices can only learn to discern, to trust, to seek, and to find the answers within through their own efforts. Of course, sometimes they will be right and sometimes they will be wrong. In either case, their faculties will be fine-tuned for the next round.

To get the right answers, however, you need to ask the right questions. Many people who start on the path are facing a major issue, or they are drowning in problems. It is therefore natural that their first concerns are aimed at resolving the issues they are facing. They want to get what they want. But this limited view can serve, over time, to keep them thinking small, looking small, and understanding small. I don't mean by this that their problems or issues are trivial or invalid. They are indeed valid and real. Unfortunately, however, the world we live in is a world focused on "fixing," and this can be an extremely dangerous approach to life, because so often, when we are focused on fixing one thing or another, we fail to see the bigger picture.

As I write this, I realize how I benefited from starting my spiritual development at an early age. Unlike most adults seeking the path, who are faced with adult problems and responsibilities, I was able to ask and develop at a time when I didn't have anything else to worry about in the physical world—no bills, no car insurance, no babysitters, no job. This allowed me to ask deeper questions sooner. Questions like:

- What is the purpose of life? What does it mean?

- Why am I here?

- How can I become connected to God?

- How can I be of service?

- What can I bring and give to the world?

ESPIRITISMO

- What do I need to do to align myself with the divine will?

- How can I be more aligned with life?

  And I was able to make sincere requests like:

- Allow me to be your servant and serve the divine will.

- Allow me to be a vessel for compassion, faith, love, and hope.

- Allow me to see your divine face and be with your divine being.

SPIRITUAL CLEANSING

One of the foundations of every *espiritista's* practice is spiritual cleansing. In Espiritismo, cleansing the spirit is just as important as bodily cleansing and hygiene. In fact, it is one of the keys to health. For mediums, spiritual cleansing is essential. Without it, they risk becoming hosts for negative energies and spirits, because working with others opens them up to these influences to a greater degree. Passes and the transfer of the *cuadro* are two techniques that experienced *espiritistas* use to cleanse themselves and others (see chapter 11). These are deep cleansings. But we can all cleanse ourselves when we know how.

One of the main practices of spiritual cleansing is the spiritual bath. Spiritual baths are not the only way to maintain good spiritual hygiene, however. Although today they are the most common means of spiritual cleansing, spiritual baths are just the tip of the iceberg when it comes to spiritual cleansing treatments. In fact, spiritual baths can have many goals. They are made by mixing various herbs and ingredients that produce the desired currents. These are mixed in water and sometimes boiled. People then either pour the mixture over themselves, or mix it in a bathtub full of water and soak in it.

There is such a thing as too much spiritual cleansing, however. If you are not a spiritual healer, you should have no need to cleanse more than once a month. If you feel the need to cleanse more often than that, something larger is at play. The same is true if you find only very temporary relief from a spiritual bath. In both cases, you should consult an *espiritista* to get help.

Here are three of my favorite spiritual baths.

Spiritual Cleansing Bath 1

This simple spiritual bath is far stronger than you may realize. Sometimes it is the simplest things that bring about the most powerful results and changes.

You will need:

• Fresh rue

• Florida Water

Boil the rue in a pot of water and say the Prayer of the Rue over top of it (see below). Then say seven Our Fathers. Allow the mixture to cool, then add it and the Florida Water to the bath. Repeat this bath for seven consecutive days.

> Prayer to the Rue Plant (translated from Spanish)
> Rue green and perfumed,

Wherever you are found, it is a sign of good luck.
Your secret is unlike any other, and never will I be without
  anything.
There is no comparison to you; you free us from all evil and
  bring us good fortune.
For your help, I bathe myself with your waters,
So that you can spill over me prosperity and luck
And keep open the door to love and money.
Amen.

Spiritual Cleansing Bath 2

This is by far one of my favorite cleansing baths. It has a double action in that it removes negativity while also giving strength. It is great when you find yourself weak, tired, and really drained. This bath is best done in the early morning if possible. Avoid taking this bath at night, because some of the ingredients can cause you to have trouble sleeping.

You will need:

- Black coffee

- 3 limes

- Florida Water

- Salt

Cut the limes in quarters, squeeze the juice into the water, and add the coffee. This can be the same kind of coffee you normally drink. Add three splashes of Florida Water. After scrubbing yourself with salt, pour this mixture over you or soak in it. This bath can be done for one, three, seven, or nine days.

Spiritual Cleansing Bath 3—White Bath

I include this bath here because it is probably the best-known and most popular of all the cleansing baths of Espiritismo. It has been incorporated into many other traditions both in and outside of the Caribbean. This bath removes bad vibes while leaving behind a clean fresh feeling.

You will need:

• Parsley

• White flower petals

• About a cup of goat's milk

• Full-fat cow's milk

• Coconut milk

• Florida Water

Mix the ingredients together and either pour the mixture over yourself or soak in it. Take this bath for three consecutive days.

PROTECTIONS

One major practice that is foundational for all *espiritistas* is the preparation and maintenance of protections. Protections push away negativity and block it from being able to affect the protected. Ultimately, the best protection is the spiritual frame, so *espiritistas* invest a lot of time, energy, and money in amplifying their *cuadros*. Protection is also important because it keeps us from having to cleanse ourselves constantly from negativity. It creates a barrier against attacks. Think of protections as shields. In fact, some *espiritistas* refer to their spirits as shields.

Energies affect us all and, just as there are positive and negative people and things in life, so are there also positive and negative spirits and forces. People attack each other spiritually just as they often attack each other in physical life. This happens in many ways. Today, many unfortunately try to ignore or deny spirituality, and this leaves them open to a host of issues and problems, among them the inability to handle, deal with, or resolve negativity. This is quite the opposite approach to that of *espiritistas*, who confront negativity head-on.

Those who are not *brujos* can go to one to have a protection given or made. In this case, the *brujo* either prepares an item that has a protective spirit attached to it, or links a protective spirit with the person's *cuadro*. In either case, the person must attend the spirit or have the *espiritista* attend it on their behalf in order to keep the protection active.

Brujos may also prepare a special item that has been made for protection, known as a *resguardo*. In this case, the item creates an actual bubble of protection around the bearer. Some *resguardos* are prepared as potions or teas for clients to drink. These protections only last for a certain amount of time, however, before they must be remade or recharged like a battery.

If you need to reverse a spiritual attack, a *brujo* can do that for you as well. *Brujos* can send negativity back to the sender without risk of being attacked themselves. This does not act as a curse, however, as they are simply sending back what was sent to you. Some *brujos* do use curses, but most do so only when they feel it is justified. It really depends on the *brujos* and their *cuadros*. Most *brujos*, however, do not take cursing lightly, because it can ruin someone's life or go on for a long time.

THE POWER TO SEE

The most powerful of all protections is *la vista*, the sight. Ironically, however, most people lose sight of this. *La vista* is the *espiritista's* power to see what is going on spiritually and communicate with the spiritual world. *La vista* can protect you more than anything else and help you navigate the waters of life. It can warn you of danger or tell you to go a different way. It can tell you what to do when you have an issue or problem, and it can direct you toward luck and open pathways.

The faculty to see is what *espiritistas* work on most consistently when they develop *la luz* and their *cuadros*. Perceptions and reality don't usually match, and *espiritistas* work to remove the framework of perception in order to be able to see reality more and more clearly. By being able to see through the layers of energies, they are guided and shown where to go and what to do.

La vista is not easy to develop, however, and it is easy to fall into the belief that it is more developed than it actually is. In fact, *espiritistas* encounter many challenges and pitfalls along the way, including assuming in error that they are seeing truth. Physical sight is one of the senses that people rely on most. They assume that what they see with their eyes, and how they interpret those perceptions with their minds, is in fact truth when it is actually just their interpretation of what they saw.

The primary tools for developing *la vista* are *la fuente* and proper prayer practices. The fountain helps to open up *facultades*, or abilities, and is also useful for scrying. Using the *fuente* to scry is a common method for encouraging *la vista* because, while scrying, you must clear your mind and keep your focus on the fountain. This is a little more complex than what I can explain here. Suffice it to say that the fountain acts in many ways to develop the sight.

Divination tools are also helpful for developing the capacity of sight, and there are as many ways to divine as there are types of trees in the world. All *espiritistas* have their preferred methods, and mediums have a great variety to choose from. Here are just a few:

- *Reading cards.* This is one the most popular forms of divination among *espiritistas.* Many read the *baraja Española,* or the Spanish playing cards. Others read regular playing cards, tarot cards, or any other type of cards.

- *Sortilegios,* or casting of lots. In the United States and elsewhere, this is often called "throwing the bones." Real bones may or may not be involved.

- *Reading cigars and cups of coffee.* This method is particularly popular among mediums. They prepare espresso coffee and serve it to their clients. Once the cup is empty, they can discern messages in the bottom of the cup. The same messages can be sought in the ashes from a cigar.

- *La clave,* or automatic writing. This method was popular among American spiritualists.

- *El huevó,* or the egg. In this technique, mediums rub their clients with an egg and then break it into a glass of water. They then read the shapes, signs, and symbols that appear.

THE *ESPIRITISTA* TOOLBOX

Contrary to popular belief, you do not need a whole arsenal of tools in order to develop yourself spiritually, work magic, or do healing work. A candle and a glass of water can and do work wonders. The most important and ultimate tool is you yourself. Your faith and honest sacrifice will take you farther spiritually than any tool ever could. In fact, investing in your training and spiritual development is sure to be more effective than any tool you can use.

If you are like most spiritualists, however, you love spiritual items and goodies, and there are plenty of them in Espiritismo. In fact, it is usually a love of these items rather than an actual need by the spirits or the work at hand that causes spiritualists to accumulate spiritual tools and materials.

There are, however, a few items that *espiritistas* commonly use. One of these is *alcoholados,* alcohol-based liquids sometimes distilled from herbs, sometimes produced as perfumes and colognes. There are many different types of these mixtures. In the case of herbal mixtures, you can easily make your own. In the case of perfumes and colognes, which are used in large amounts, you can simply use commercial products, which are both cost-effective and widely available.

Another common tool is a seven-day glass-encased candle. These candles are usually eight to nine inches tall and encased in a glass. Sometimes the candle can be pulled out, and this is known as a pull-out. These candles are often seen on Catholic altars. Many people think there is something special about them, and I agree that they do give off a very magical vibe, but they are not really special. You can just as easily use pillar candles whenever you need a candle of that size. In fact, some pillar candles are already scented, which can be beneficial. Just match the scent, color, and intention of the candle.

There are some tools that are worth investing in—for instance, some nice glassware and candle holders for your altars. Just make sure that you do not use glass candle holders, as these are known to crack and can cause a fire. Some nice altar cloths are also useful, as are images, statues, or dolls for your guides, your patron saint, and other *protecciones*. A rosary, religious symbols, and an incense burner can come in handy, and I also recommend an enamelware basin, cups, and pitcher if possible. All these items can be immensely helpful to you in doing many types of rituals. Many of them can be obtained very cheaply, even at secondhand stores.

The following prayer books are also commonly used by *espiritistas* in their work:

- The Bible

- *La Fe en La Oracion*

- *Helping Yourself with Selected Prayers, Volumes 1 and II*

- Oraciones Escogidas

Here are some of the most common supplies you will want to keep on hand and restock often.

- White candles

- Florida Water

- Various *alcoholados* (for example, rue water, open-road water, Don Dinero)

- Candles of various colors

- Incense

- Herbs

The truth is that you do not really need a whole bunch of exotic and specialty items to work Espiritismo, although many people think they do and this can keep them moving forward. Elders often joke that, when people first start on the path, they want to go to the *botanica* all the time and buy all kinds of things. Once on the path, however, they find that they rarely have need to go there and go instead to the grocery store, the craft store, and the dollar store. In fact, aside from certain herbs—which, especially when being used medicinally, must be exact—most of the items *espiritistas* need can be obtained very easily.

When *botanicas* were first established, they sold large amounts of natural herbs. That is why they were called *botanicas*. Over time, however, they have changed and now many of them sell mainly commercial products that are chemically based and have little to no natural herbal component. In fact, as of this writing, many *botanicas* only stock and carry these mass-produced items and handle very few natural products.

ALL DEBTS MUST BE PAID

It was a few minutes after 6:00 PM. We had just eaten dinner and were getting ready to go a *velada* at Tia Irma's house about twenty minutes away. Tia Irma held *sessiones* twice a month in a small garage that had been converted into a temple space. When Berta, Mercedes, and I arrived at her house dressed all in white, we were ushered into the kitchen and sat around the table there to wait.

"Tonight is going to be an incredibly special night," Berta said as she sipped her coffee. Interrupting the conversation, my cousin Manny came in through the kitchen doorway. Manny, a heavy-set but tall young man with dark hair that covered his head and spilled onto his forehead, had just started an apprenticeship with Doña Irma.

Doña Irma and her mediums had already set up much of the space, with a little table to the right-hand side of the door that held a white basin filled with perfumed water so everyone who entered could cleanse themselves spiritually. Plumes of smoke rose from a censer and each person had to cross over this in order to enter the space and then stand in front of a medium who passed his hands over our heads and shoulders, never touching us, while he mumbled a short prayer. Manny was there to direct participants to their seats.

Chairs were set up in rows that all faced a long white table where Doña Irma was seated, with two empty chairs flanking her for my aunts, Nereida and Berta. Three mediums sat to one side of them and four sat to the other side. These were Doña Irma's *ahijados* (assistants).

On the altar were cigars, a bouquet of white flowers, a huge fishbowl filled with clear water, a stack of prayer books, a Bible, a bell, and a white candle. Behind the mediums, there was a short shelf that you could barely see filled with bottles of perfumes, rum, various potions and concoctions, and a plate stacked with fresh herbs. Painted on the wall behind it was a huge all-seeing eye in a triangle with a crucifix under it. Around the room were many shelves with saints on them, some of which I recognized and others I had yet to learn about. In one corner, a bunch of canes, machetes, crutches, and other sticks leaned up against the wall, while in another corner was another table that held statutes of African slaves and dolls with candles lit before them.

In the corner farthest from me, statues of Indians sat on the floor. Here, the greatest number of candles burned, and this was the one altar that held not only many glasses of water, but also black coffee, beer, and rum. There were pipes with tobacco and cigars all nicely set in a crescent shape before the main statue—an Indian lunging forward with a long spear.

Once everyone was seated and we were ready to commence, Manny took a seat at the back of the room. Doña Irma picked up a small silver bell and rang it to signal that the *velada* was about to commence. After a few moments, Don Ileo began to read the prayers, after which Doña Irma stood up and gave a little speech.

"*Buenas noches, hermanos y hermanas* (Good evening, brothers and sisters)," she began. "Tonight we have come together to work the *causas*, to make a battle for our lives, our souls, and our families. Evil is strong, but God is stronger than any evil, and so we come together in the name of God and the good spirits to improve our roads."

Irma resumed her seat and Don Ileo asked for the *union de pensamientos*. After a moment or two, the congregation was instructed to begin praying the Our Father.

As we repeated the prayer, the mediums called upon their *cuadros*. One by one, they began to shake and jerk violently, while passing their hands over their heads and shoulders. Each one spoke a greeting, after which their bodies relaxed.

Doña Irma pointed at a woman sitting several rows behind me and said: "You have an infernal spirit with you. You're not able to rest or sleep. Come to the front." The young woman nodded her head and said "luz," confirming what Doña Irma had told her.

"You've been feeling that you can't sit still or feel at peace, especially in your home," Irma continued. "You feel more and more irritated as each member of your family arrives home at the end of the day. This just started to happen in the last month or so. And you've been asking yourself what's wrong with you. You know something is wrong, but you feel you can't help it.

"Your husband irritates you most of all, yet he hasn't changed one bit. There's nothing specific that you can complain about with his character or behavior. But for whatever reason, you can't seem to stop feeling more and more agitated and frustrated when he talks. This has caused unnecessary and stupid drama in your home. Clearly an intranquil spirit is tormenting you. Have you been having dreams that your husband is cheating on you? It isn't happening yet, but it will if you continue on in this way."

The woman's face showed signs of both surprise and relief, and she started crying gently. Immediately, Doña Irma set to the task of drawing the offending spirit out. Still facing the woman, she began speaking with it.

"Spirit, you dirty spirit who torments this girl, show yourself. You like to hide there and twist her mind, but, as strong as you are, you are too afraid to come out. May spirits of light draw you forward."

"And union of thoughts, union of thoughts," one of the mediums cried out, instructing the congregation to join in prayer so their concentrated fluids and collective light could support the work that was being done.

Another medium at the table started to quiver—softly at first, then more and more violently, breathing heavily and hands shaking as he passed the dark spirit. All through this process, the congregation continued to pray in unison. Once the dark spirit had gained enough control to speak, it made its presence known.

"What the hell," the spirit screeched. "What do you want from me? If it's not one thing, it's another. Shit!"

"*No venga aqui con tus maldiciones* (Don't come here cursing)," Doña Irma retorted. "What are you doing with this girl? What do you want with her? You think you're helping yourself but you're not."

"I'm innocent," the spirit protested. "She herself called me here. She herself asked for me."

"What? What do you mean?" Irma asked.

"She did a *trabajo* on that man. She lit candles for him. She knew he was not for her, but she did it anyway. And she didn't pay me."

When Irma turned to the woman for confirmation, she nodded reluctantly. The spirit was telling the truth. She didn't know that she had to pay him, she said. She didn't know that the man was not for her, she said. She didn't know her actions would have these consequences, she said.

"Liar," the spirit spat back. "She was ungrateful and never intended to pay."

"But you are only hurting yourself in the long run," Irma countered. "You are only delaying your own suffering. With or without you, she will pay for what she has done. All debts must be paid. That is the law. All you are doing is slowing yourself down and robbing yourself of peace by tormenting her. You are harming yourself more than you are harming her."

"I don't care," the spirit shot back. "I'm owed what I am owed, and she needs to pay. *Lo que se hace se paga* (What one does, one pays for)."

"What can she give to you that will lift you from your suffering?" Doña Irma asked. "She is there suffering with you. We have come to help both of you. To give you relief from your suffering. We have the light to feed you with."

"I still want what I want," the spirit growled.

"What is it that you want?"

"I want her blood."

"She cannot give you that," Irma argued. "But she can offer you prayers and light. She can make a *novena* and give you three *Misas*. You can take this and go in peace, or we can send you to *escuela espiritual*. But you will not keep your hold over her."

Then, turning to the woman, Irma said: "Do you see how this spirit is suffering? Can you forgive him for what he has done to you?" The woman nodded her head. "Will you give him what I said you would?" The woman agreed.

"She will forgive you," Irma said, "but you must forgive her in return. This will bring you much good and help you progress on your journey."

The spirit remained quiet at first, but then began to cry and nod. "Yes, yes, I will take it and go. But she must pay it. And quickly. I am not going to go if she takes too long."

Doña Irma assured him that would not be a problem and the medium who had been hosting the spirit began to relax and slumped over. "*Luz y progresso*," he said hoarsely, allowing his *cuadro* to come through and clear him out.

After that difficult negotiation, the *sessione* moved along more quickly. A young man of about thirty was hearing voices that he could not silence. He had been to see medical doctors and had been to other *espiritistas*, but nothing seemed to help. Irma diagnosed his problem as a karmic burden he had assumed in his late teens. She called on the man's aunt, who had raised him and was present, to help heal him, warning him that he would be entering into an agreement with his *cuadro*, an agreement that must be honored. "All debts must be paid," she warned him as he returned to his seat.

Then another medium pointed to a young woman of about twenty-five and said: "You don't sleep at night. They don't let you. You feel their presence all night." The woman nodded as she came somewhat nervously up to the front.

"These *causas* have been sent to destroy you," the medium warned. Apparently the woman had experienced a number of setbacks, including the loss of a

good-paying job for which she had not really been quali-
fied. The medium told her that malign spirits had set her
up for failure and performed black magic on her. She
would require a special cleansing in order to free herself
from these negative energies.

Throughout the evening, messages and healing continued to come through for those in the congregation.
Right before the end, another medium began to tremble
lightly and pass through another spirit.

"*Buenas noches, hermanos,*" said the rusty voice of an
old man. This spirit, who was one of the medium's guides,
had come to give a cleansing and a blessing to the people. He called various people up and proceeded to cleanse
them with hand passes and Florida Water as he made the
sign of the cross over them. Then he turned to the congregation and said: "May the Light stay with you all."

"And with you," the congregation responded.

Then the closing prayers were recited and everyone
filed out. Once outside the ritual space, the congregation
snacked on cheese and crackers, drank coffee, and spoke
about general things, as it was forbidden to speak of the
events of the evening outside of the ritual space unless it
was for the purpose of teaching. The mediums retired to a
bedroom where they also snacked and talked. Once members of the congregation had left, they gathered at the
dining room table where they were joined by Manny, who
reviewed the impressions and *videncias* he had received
during the ritual.

CONCLUSION

Con Dios venimos y con Dios nos vamos (With God we came and with God we'll go).

Puerto Rican proverb

Here God comes along again. Many lose sight of God while walking on the spiritual path. Espiritismo is a big and beautiful tradition, with many interesting spirits, tools, and workings. Thus it can be quite easy to lose sight of its main focus. But if you lose sight of God, you lose your way.

Since the beginning of my life, all my *madrinas* and *padrinos* have put a strong and continual focus on God, reminding me that God is what our spiritual practice is all about. Above and beyond the spirits, the rituals, the tools, and everything else, it is God for whom we work. It is God's will with which we align. It is God we seek and, if God is willing, it is God we will find. The spirits and the work are all just tools to help us get closer and closer to God.

Espiritismo is like Puerto Rican yoga, to me. The true goal of yoga is to unite with the Divine. Espiritismo is one of the few spiritual traditions of the West that seeks to bring about union between the individual and the whole.

So, I leave you with a message from one of my guides, Don Nico:

Con Dios delante y Dios atras, nunca moriras. (With God before you and God behind you, you will never die.)

GLOSSARY

ahijados: apprentices of an elder *espiritista* who is training and in development.

alcoholados: alcohol-based perfumes and colognes.

angel custodio: guardian angel.

Arabes: group of spirit guides originating in Arabia.

assistentes: another term for spirit guides.

barridas: cleansing or healing a person by means of sweeping herbs and other items across the body.

behique: Taino term for shaman.

bodega: small Hispanic convenience store.

Borinquen: Taino word for the island of Puerto Rico and its people.

botanica: spiritual and magical supply store.

boveda: ancestral altar common in Cuban Espiritismo, now also used among Puerto Rican *espiritistas*.

brujeria: witchcraft, used positively or negatively depending on the person and context.

brujo: professional *espiritista* who does magic and healing for others, used positively or negatively depending on the person and context.

cacique: Taino chief.

cadena: group of spirit guides, also called courts and commissions.

casilla: term used to refer to a medium by the spirits.

causas de nacimiento: negative entities and karma that are present at birth.

causas: negative entities that wreak havoc and cause illness.

cemi: Taino god or spirit guide; also the stone or material in which the god or spirit guide lives.

centro: temple or meeting place, usually a separate structure, where *espiritistas* practice Espiritismo.

Chamanes: group of spirit guides that consists of shamans.

Chango: African deity of the Santeria pantheon associated with power and strength.

clave: automatic writing or the use of writing in magical works and divination.

commission Santera: group of spirit guides connected with Santeria.

commission: term used to describe a group of spirit guides, also called courts and chains.

corriente: emissions of energy given off by every spirit.

Criollos (Creoles): people of mixed Spanish and Taino blood.

cruzado: to be hexed or cursed; to be "crossed up" or blocked.

cuadro spiritual: spiritual frame that contains all the spirits, karma, and light that a person has.

curandero: healer.

darle luz: practices designed to give light and strength to the spirits; also refers to burning a candle for a spirit.

demonios: evil spirits who harm humanity.

desarrollo: the process of spiritual development.

despojandose: cleansing oneself through spiritual passes or baths.

difuntos: the dead, ancestors.

djinn: spirits of Islamic and pre-Islamic religions.

Eleggua: African deity of the Santeria pantheon associated with crossroads and doors; often represented by a small cement head behind a door.

embrujiado: bewitched, cursed.

emissions: energetic discharges that are released by people and spirits.

Encantos: group of spirit guides who never lived.

encausado: victim of a cause or negative spirit.

ensalmar: to cast a magical spell; to bless or protect by spiritual means.

ensalmos: psalms and prayers used in spells or magical works.

enviacion: to send a spirit against an enemy or another person.

Esclavos: group of spirit guides who were slaves in life.

escuela spiritual: spiritual school to which spirits are sent by more evolved spirits when they need to be educated and helped to progress.

espiriteros: derogatory term used by Kardecists to ridicule and belittle *espiritistas* of the Mesa Blanca tradition.

Espiritismo Cruzado: Mesa Blanca Espiritismo mixed with other Afro-Caribbean religions and spiritualities.

Espiritismo: group of practices and traditions that believe in God, the realms of spirits, and the interactions and communications between spirits and man.

espiritista: practitioner and follower of Espiritismo.

espiritu amarrado: spirit who keeps someone from being able to do anything about a life situation; also refers to the victim of such a spirit.

espiritu atrasado: spirit who causes setbacks and is degressing rather than progressing; also refers to the victim of such a spirit.

espiritu burlone: spirit who mocks, ridicules, and makes fun of its victims.

espiritu de arrastre: spirit who seeks to drag its victims through life and cause constant turmoil.

espiritu de causa: negative spirit who causes suffering in those to whom it attaches.

espiritu de confusion: spirit who causes confusion in its victims.

espiritu de luz: good spirit who seeks to help others evolve and progress.

espiritu de rabia, odio, y ira: spirit that causes rage, hate, and anger in its victims.

espiritu intranquilo: spirit who causes anxiety, unsteadiness, and a lack of peace and tranquility in its victims.

facultades: spiritual abilities that mediums use to communicate and work with the spirits.

fuente: glass or bowl of water central to all altars and tables used in Espiritismo rituals.

fuerza: a person's personal or spiritual power.

Gitanas y Gitanos: group of spirit guides known as Gypsies.

guia material: elder developed *espiritista* who is the physical living guide to a novice *espiritista*.

guia personal: personal spirit guide who is connected to a specific person.

guia principal: the main spirit guide of an individual.

guias falsos: negative spirit guides who falsely direct victims toward devolving and suffering.

hacer caridad: to give to charity or to help others without compensation.

Indias: group of spirit guides made up of female Taino Indians and Native Americans.

Indios bravos: aggressive Indians.

Indios de la paz: Indians of peace.

Indios de la pluma blanca: White feather Indians; also refers to all other types of Indians not categorized elsewhere.

Indios del agua: Indians of water.

Indios del monte: Indians of the woods.

Indios guerreros: warrior Indians.

Indios: group of spirit guides made up of male Taino Indians and Native Americans.

jibaros: country people, farmers.

Juanes y Marias (Johns and Marys): group of spirit guides made up of natives converted by the Catholic Church.

kolonias: alcohol-based colognes.

Kongos: group of spirit guides made up of Africans brought to the Caribbean from the Congo.

lava pisos: mixture of herbs, perfumes, and other materials used to wash the floors of a home and purify it spiritually.

levantamiento: ritual used to uplift someone, to heal, or to increase spiritual power.

levantando los muertos: rituals done to uplift or remove spirits of the dead who are causing problems for a living person.

limpieza: rituals of various forms to cleanse and remove negativity or negative spirits.

luces oscuras: negative spirits.

Lucumi: Cuban religious tradition that honors and serves the orishas, African deities of the Yoruba people; also known as Santeria.

luz: light, spiritual power.

Madamas: group of spirit guides made up of deceased nannies and African slave women who took care of the house and children.

Madamos: group of spirit guides made up of deceased African slave men who served as assistants and butlers.

madrina: female mentor and teacher.

mal de ojo (evil eye): negativity and jealousy projected toward another that causes harm.

mayores: experienced and developed *espiritistas,* elder spiritual guides who can help others.

medicos: doctors.

Mesa Blanca (white table): name of the spirituality of Puerto Rican Espiritismo; also used to refer to the altars in that tradition.

mesa espiritual: personal altar to honor an individual's spirits.

mi muerto (my dead), tu muerto (your dead): a person's spirit guides or the dead spirits that help them.

Misa: ritual of Espiritismo designed to communicate messages from the spirits to the living.

misterios: spirits of the tradition of the 21 Divisions of the Dominican Republic.

montar los seres: to be taken over by the spirits and used as a vehicle for communication.

muerteros or muerteras: *espiritistas* who have the ability to work with the dead (male and female respectively).

muertos: the dead.

muñeca: dolls used in Espiritismo to house spirits and guides.

Negras y Africanas: group of spirit guides made up of Black and African women.

novena: nine-day prayer ritual.

Obatala: African deity of the Santeria pantheon associated with peace and purity.

Ogun: African deity of the Santeria pantheon associated with war and iron.

Orientales: group of Asian spirit guides.

orishas: African deities of the Yoruba people of modern-day Nigeria.

Oshun: African deity of the Santeria pantheon associated with love.

Oya: African deity of the Santeria pantheon associated with cemeteries and the dead.

padrino: male teacher and mentor.

Palo Mayombe: spiritual tradition from Cuba with foundations in the heritage of the Congo people of Africa.

pasar los seres: to be used as a vessel by the spirits and possessed.

patrones: a person's main spirits.

pendiente: watchfulness that brings about negativity and becomes a source of potential problems.

Piratas y Marineros: group of spirit guides made up of deceased pirates and sailors.

presidente: leader of spiritual rituals in Espiritismo.

protecciones: spirit guides who protect *espiritistas*.

pruebas: trials and tribulations.

Religiosos: group of spirit guides who were priests in some form or another.

reunion espiritual: one of the main rituals of Espiritismo, conducted for communication between the living and the spirits (also known as a Misa).

sabiendo: a spiritual knowing without any rational basis.

salado: negative condition that causes a person to repel other people.

sanaciónes: healings or healing rituals.

Sanse: spiritual tradition that blends Mesa Blanca Espiritismo and 21 Divisions.

Santeria: Cuban spiritual tradition that honors and serves the African deities of the Yoruba people, known as orishas.

Santerismos: blended practice of Santeria and Mesa Blanca.

santeristas: practitioners of Santerismo.

santeros: priests of Santeria; often improperly used to mean anyone practicing any spiritual tradition or religion; used in the past to refer to people who made statues of saints out of wood.

santiguar: healing ritual in which a person is prayed over and has the sign of the cross drawn over them.

santos de bulto: statues of Catholic saints carved from wood.

santos: saints, including Catholic saints.

seres: spirits.

sessiones: Spiritist meetings, rituals, and reunions (see reunion espiritual and Misa).

Siete Potencias: Seven African Powers; refers to the seven most popular deities of Santeria.

sortilegios: casting of lots, also called throwing of the bones.

trabajar las causas: to heal by removing negative spirits.

trabajo: spiritual work or rituals.

trabajos buenos: spiritual rituals or spells that work toward good ends.

trabajos de limpieza: rituals and spells to cleanse and remove negativity.

trabajos de luz: rituals and spells considered white magic that work toward positive ends.

trabajos de sanación: healing works.

trabajos malos: spells and rituals of black magic.

traer una luz: bring a light, bring a candle.

trance asombrao: trance in which a medium is overshadowed by a spirit, but is completely conscious of the events.

trance inconsiente: trance in which a medium loses all control and recollection.

trance media unidad: trance in which a medium retains some control and recollection of the events during the trance.

union de pensamientos: praying together with a single purpose or goal.

velada de desenvolvimiento: candle ritual devoted to bringing about evolution and progress.

velada: candle-based ritual.

videncia: information given to mediums by the spirits that can be proven as fact.

videntes: clairivoyants.

viejos: old ones or elders; term used to describe elevated spiritual guides or elder *espiritistas*.

vista: the ability to see things spiritually.

Vodou: religion of African slaves and their desendants in Haiti.

Yemaya: African deity of the Santeria pantheon associated with the sea.

ABOUT THE AUTHOR

Hector Salva was born into a family lineage of brujos (witchdoctors, healers, sorcerers). Raised by his grandmother, Doña Juana Acevedo, a *bruja* and *espiritista,* he is the author of *The 21 Divisions: Mysteries and Magic of Dominican Voodoo,* and his writing has been featured in a number of publications. He has also been initiated into Haitian Voodoo as a *houngan asogwe,* a high priest of the Asson lineage. Follow him on Instagram @brujo21division.

TO OUR READERS